Condos, Co-ops, & Townhomes

A Complete Guide to Finding, Buying, Maintaining, and Enjoying Your New Home

MARK B. WEISS, CCIM

Dearborn™
Trade Publishing
A **Kaplan Professional** Company

This publication is designed to provide accurate and authoritative information in regard to the subject matter covered. It is sold with the understanding that the publisher is not engaged in rendering legal, accounting, or other professional service. If legal advice or other expert assistance is required, the services of a competent professional should be sought.

Vice President and Publisher: Cynthia A. Zigmund
Acquisitions Editor: Mary B. Good
Senior Project Editor: Trey Thoelcke
Interior Design: Lucy Jenkins
Cover Design: Jody Billert
Typesetting: Elizabeth Pitts

Published by Dearborn Trade Publishing, a Kaplan Professional Company

Printed in the United States of America

03 04 05 10 9 8 7 6 5 4 3 2 1

Library of Congress Cataloging-in-Publication Data

Weiss, Mark B.
    Condos, co-ops, and townhomes : a complete guide to finding, buying, maintaining, and enjoying your new home / Mark B. Weiss.
        p. cm.
Includes index.
    ISBN 0-7931-7840-1
    1. House buying. 2. Real estate business. 3. Real property.   I. Title.
HD1379.W357 2003
643′.12–dc21

                                                              2003014469

Dearborn Trade Publishing books are available at special quantity discounts to use for sales promotions, employee premiums, or educational purposes. Please contact our special sales department, to order or for more information, at trade@dearborn.com or 800-245 BOOK (2665), or write to Dearborn Financial Publishing, 30 South Wacker Drive, Suite 2500, Chicago, IL 60606-7481.

I dedicate this book to anyone who recognizes opportunity and is not afraid to greet it, to those who realize obstacles can simply be overcome, and to people who are never afraid to take responsibility for their actions and behaviors.

"By being a responsible person who overcomes the challenges of life, you will be cheerfully overwhelmed with opportunity and memorable life experiences."

Mark B. Weiss

Contents

PART FOUR

BEYOND THE MOVE-IN

Although this book may be long forgotten or overlooked in future generations, it is an important work to those of you reading it now. You are entering the most exciting time of your life—home ownership. I have prepared a complete guide to the stepping stones toward your success. I'm sharing my own experiences to guide you to the right way to buy your home and make your dreams come true. I truly and sincerely hope the book is helpful to you and look forward to your letting me know how successful you have been.

This book was written as a step-by-step, start-to-finish guidebook for buying a condo, townhome, or co-op as a primary residence. As a new homeowner, or even as an investor, you are entering one of the most exciting times of your life, especially those of you planning to make that dramatic and joyous transition from renter to homeowner. Here you will discover that association living is the most affordable way to enter the market. More than that, you will discover how to go about it, how to avoid the pitfalls, and how to take advantage of the many and sometimes easy-to-overlook opportunities readily available to you.

My first home was a condominium, and it provided me with pride of ownership, allowed me to build equity, and live in a great Chicago community. I welcome you enthusiastically to the exclusive club of homeownership.

I've written this book because during the past 15 years, homebuyers have begun to realize the value of owning townhomes, condos, and co-ops. This trend is accelerating throughout the United States and Canada. Clearly, a need exists for a book to guide first-time homebuyers and investors through the complex and often confusing process of buying their first home. This is a practical, in-depth, and reader-friendly book designed to help ease the way for these first-time buyers and investors into the wonderful world of homeownership.

If you are one of them, congratulations!

This dedication is an expression of thanks and gratitude made publicly to recognize people who have assisted me throughout my life, not only in my writing career, but in other areas of my life as well.

First, I want to tell my wife, Marilyn, that I love her and thank her for her unconditional support and generosity of love throughout our life together. Having you, Marilyn, has allowed me the freedom of mind to pursue the challenges that have been presented to me.

I have the best son in the world, Daniel Mark Egel-Weiss. I love watching you grow and develop. You are becoming a fine young man, and you always make me proud with your thinking, observations of life, and passion. You're *It*!

To my parents, Alvin and Flora Weiss; you have great energy and I respect your selflessness as you are always doing things for others. I hope you know that I love you and that the experiences we have shared are precious moments to me.

To my grandparents, who never lived to see this day, I will always remember their influence on my life, and I hope that somehow they can see or sense my accomplishment.

I want to thank a wonderful writer, Dan Baldwin. Dan, you are a terrific writer, and I need you on my team to put my words and stories together in an entertaining format that readers can and will enjoy. I recommend you highly as a skillful man who deserves much recognition.

And to Kathy Welton, without whose vision I would never have had the opportunity I have today. Thanks.

I want to acknowledge the following people who have helped me throughout the years in buying, understanding, developing, and selling condominiums and association properties:

The Lincoln Park Builders of Chicago

Perry Peterson	Dan Lowenstein	Art Evans
Mark Pearlstein	Faye Pantazelos	Richard Wexner
Terry Engel	Abe Triger	Avrum Reifer
Dan Starzyk	Steve Olsen	Peter Haleas
Ryan Cooley	Brian Griffin	Abe Trieger
Liza Bachrach	Jerry Jakubco	Wayne Zuschlag

The Chicago Association of Realtors

FIRST STEPS

1

WHY A CONDOMINIUM, CO-OP, OR TOWNHOME?

"Opportunity is as scarce as oxygen;
men fairly breath it and do not know it."

Doc Sane

OPPORTUNITY IS IN THE AIR

The opportunity to own a home, even for young first-timers, is everywhere. Home ownership may not be as "free as the air," but, like oxygen, it's out there, so breathe it in. Association products—condominiums, co-operatives, and townhomes—are excellent choices for starter homes. They're sound investments, comfortable, affordable, and full of amenities. Association housing is also a great stepping stone to larger properties later in life. As more and more people realize these facts, association living is becoming more and more popular. (You'll find some interesting statistics on this subject in later chapters.) Because you're reading this book, I assume that you have made the decision to purchase association housing or you are at least interested in that terrific opportunity. Good choice!

Most of us will live in three to four houses during our lifetime, a break with tradition. Our parents' generation generally lived in two homes during a lifetime, a starter home and the second home in which they lived the rest of their life. Prior to that, many generations often lived in and inherited the same property. An associate of mine just sold the family farm. The kids are scattered around the country, and no one can afford to live in, or keep up, the old homestead, even though that farm has been in the family since the 1850s. The modern world has radically changed the old ways of living.

My parents lived in a rental apartment during the 1950s. Their first true house was a co-op built for returning GIs after World War II. As the family grew, we moved into the typical American Dream home: three-bedrooms, one-and-a-half baths, a yard, and close proximity to my school. We lived a true mid-twentieth-century lifestyle. Dads played catch with their sons in the front yards while moms and their daughters practiced domestic tranquility with an Easy Bake oven. It was a great life.

Unfortunately, that lifestyle is virtually impossible for today's young families. Affordable single-family homes in urban areas are as common as living dinosaurs. That's one of many reasons so many young people are choosing association housing. That's not a lowering of standards or expectations either. As you'll see, condos, co-ops, and townhomes are wonderful financial and lifestyle investments. Many singles already living in condos choose to sell them when they get married and move into a townhome, especially true if they live in a city like Chicago. Association living has many, many advantages.

Before we go any further, let's settle on a few basic definitions. *Barron's Real Estate Handbook* defines a *condominium,* or "condo," as a system of ownership of individual units in a multiunit structure combined with joint ownership of commonly used property such as sidewalks, hallways, and stairs.

A *cooperative,* or "co-op," is defined as housing in which each tenant is a shareholder in the corporation owning the building.

A *townhome* is a dwelling, usually with two or more floors, attached to other similar units by common walls called "party walls."

What's the difference?

Condos and co-ops are quite different. When purchasing a condo, you're truly buying real estate—solid property that you can touch, such as walls, floors, and ceilings—but you do not purchase the land. When you buy a co-op, you're not buying land or property; you're buying shares in a company as if you were buying shares of GE, Ford, Microsoft, or AT&T, mutual funds, or your brother-in-law's perpetual motion machine. You may live on the property, but you don't really own the specific roof over your head, the dirt beneath your floor, or the space around you. Taxes are paid by the property owner, which is the corporation, although this expense is passed on as part of your monthly rent. Of course, it's deductible on your income tax. As a corporation, a co-op has a board of directors with the power to approve or reject potential investors according to the individual or family's income level or personal character. The board cannot make decisions, however, that violate the nation's civil rights laws. We'll return to this subject shortly.

Townhomes and condos have much in common; in fact, in many cases townhomes are designated condominiums under the law. Owners of townhomes generally, although not always, own the land on which their property rests. Also, most townhomes are two-story structures.

AFFORDABLE OPPORTUNITY

Francis Bacon once said, "If a man looks sharply and attentively, he shall see Fortune; for though she is blind, she is not invisible." Bacon also said that "the mold of a man's fortune is in his hands." Fortune, in the form of affordable housing, is neither invisible nor out of your grasp. Don't listen to all the negativity out there about the economy, the availability of quality housing in your community, or the impossibility of young people's ability to buy a good first home. Listen instead to the sound advice and proven strategies in this book.

Fortune is an applicable word when applied to association housing. According to the National Association of Realtors, condominium prices have risen 23 percent at an annual rate of 5.1 percent since 1996. By comparison, new home prices rose 21 percent and existing home prices rose 20 percent.[1] Many real estate experts predict that the comparatively low price of condos will continue to attract buyers for some time. For example, the median 2001 price for an existing condo was $122,600 compared with a median of $147,500 for a single family dwelling. Clearly, ease of entry into the market and appreciation of that investment is a primary factor in the rising popularity of association housing.

I think it's important for you to understand how association housing became the affordable choice in this day and age. In the 1950s, the United States experienced the highest rate of home ownership in the history of the world. We tend to set that kind of record here. Many returning GIs found that their old home-town jobs had, by necessity, been given to other men and women. Other GIs found that jobs had moved to other cities or other parts of the country. Still others discov-

that the jobs had been eliminated by an amazing burst of technological progress.

Many of the GIs headed for "the big city" and the sights they'd been introduced to during training and shipment to and from the fronts. Urban locations offered many attractions such as entertainment and cultural opportunities. More than that, they offered jobs. This exodus was in part spurred by the government through the GI bill.

The GI Bill Act of June 22, 1944, was created to help America's war veterans get a shot at a better life and a leg up on an improved lifestyle. It was signed into law by President Franklin Roosevelt on June 22, 1944. The bill had many features, among which were (1) helping veterans return to civilian life; (2) providing educational opportunities to those who could not afford them; (3) restoring educational opportunities that had been lost or sacrificed to the war effort; (4) providing vocational assistance to servicemen and servicewomen who lost or sacrificed employment to serve their country; (5) enhancing the all-volunteer postwar military; (6) encouraging reenlistment; (7) promoting a stronger nation through a better-educated and better-employed workforce. The government also instituted lower interest rates to spur the economy.

It worked and it worked well. Some have said that the GI Bill had the most profound impact on America since the post–Civil War Homestead Act. World War II and the worldwide Great Depression before it had created an absence of homebuyers. Suddenly, a rush to home ownership and independence by a large number of people in their 20s and 30s characterized the postwar years. Loans to veterans, low interest rates, and other incentives provided more power for the economic engine. Developers who had acquired cheap land in areas that had previously been agricultural communities began to see greater profits in building homes for the returning GIs and their families. Low costs and high demand created a housing boom unequaled in the free world.

Until that time, most young families gravitated toward rental housing, which was all they could really afford. After the war, the government moved in a big way to stimulate an economy still reeling from the Great Depression. There was a boom in almost all sectors of the market, especially housing. Remember that housing includes not only finished homes but also land, concrete, wood, shingles, plumbing, electrical wiring, nails, tools, and a new workforce back from overseas looking for jobs. Home ownership and independence were no longer dreams to be deferred but a reality to be grasped at the moment. Francis Bacon was right; a man's fortune was at last right there in his hands.

AFFORDABLE HOUSING BECOMES THE NORM

Jump ahead to the present. Now, for two generations we've grown up knowing, living, and expecting to live someday in our own home. We take it for granted, but many people don't realize that things were very different just a few decades ago.

Things changed after the war, and they kept on changing. Today, it's virtually a waste of time for a single family to seek an affordable single-family detached dwelling with a yard in urban areas. Families have moved to the suburbs, and most of the businesses serving them followed. Some farsighted businesspeople even led the way. "If we build it, they will come." The exodus to the suburbs left a lot of unused and unwanted real estate downtown.

Then things changed again, as they always do. During the late sixties and early seventies, a group of Americans loosely identified as "hippies" began to move back into the city. They rejected their parents' suburban lifestyle to create their own. Being on the low end of the economic strata as recently graduated college students or young people just entering the workforce, they looked for bargains in living quarters. All of that empty downtown space provided a strong draw. Those old Victorian homes abandoned by their parents became very attractive for a number of good reasons.

Downtown offered clubs, music, proximity to libraries and schools, a certain "electricity," and lots of housing space at affordable prices. Landlords were delighted to find a group of people willing to pay good money to live in those vintage dwellings that had been pretty much left to the minorities who couldn't make the transition to suburban life. It was your traditional win-win situation for owners and renters.

Chicago is a perfect example. One of its neighborhoods—Lincoln Park—is on the outskirts of downtown, or the Loop, and a few blocks from Lake Michigan just west of one of the finest park districts in the world. During the early part of the 20th century, Lincoln Park's numerous Victorian houses provided homes for the city's working poor. After

World War II, the out-movement of parents to the suburbs was to a significant extent reversed by their sons and daughters, who wanted their own share of independence.

Slowly, and sometimes kicking, biting, and scratching all the way, these hippies soon wanted to upgrade their lifestyle, so they started improving their living quarters. Over time they renovated, redeveloped, and invested money to improve the quality of vintage buildings and make them more fit for a contemporary way of living. As the buildings, blocks, and neighborhoods improved, the residents began to realize what a great community they had built. Instead of moving out as their parents had done, they stayed put. They aged. They sought and obtained better employment. They earned more money and were soon seeking ways to put excess capital to work. Hippies became yuppies.

Yuppies—young urban professionals—helped create an infrastructure within the city of Chicago. They had earlier been social activists, a habit that didn't change. As yuppies, they pressed the city government for better schools, better streets, better parks and amenities, and better service from their government.

I am one of those people—one who moved into Lincoln Park in the early seventies. During those years I lived in an apartment building with generous one-bedroom units. I paid $275 a month for a large four-room, one-bedroom, first-floor Victorian apartment; approximately 56 units were in that building. While I lived there, the property was sold three times.

Property owners were again realizing a tidy profit from previously abandoned buildings. During the seventies, a lot of buildings were going up throughout America, and the price of land was going up right along with the buildings. New types of dwellings made of steel and glass were part of the trend. The new types were apartment-style buildings called condominiums, or condos. Then a light bulb went off, and owners realized a way to make a bigger profit from the same property, a better way to capitalize on their investment.

Smart owners with vintage buildings in city neighborhoods realized they could renovate apartments, add contemporary finishes, and sell the units individually by creating condominium associations. This was another win-win situation. Property owners could realize a sizeable profit while still providing the opportunity for home ownership to individuals and families in the community. Today, the condo is a common, well-accepted, and popular form of housing from coast to coast, that's getting more popular all the time.

NEW LIFE FOR AN OLD TRADITION

Townhomes have been a part of American culture for hundreds of years. If you have the opportunity to travel to or vacation on our eastern seaboard, make time to tour the historic parts of the cities, especially cities in Virginia, Massachusetts, New York, Rhode Island, and other New England states. You'll soon see that attached housing or row houses of two stories were our first form of townhomes. Not only did the Founding Fathers create a nation, but they also founded a lifestyle that continues today.

After World War II, the population grew at an accelerated pace, the origin of the baby boom generation. Men returning from the war and wives waiting for them wanted to start families and begin claiming their share of the American dream. Owning a home was a big part of that dream. As the cities spread, agricultural land became too valuable for agriculture. The real money was being made in land development.

Row upon row of townhomes were built to accommodate the growing World War II–era and Korean conflict–era families. These dwellings became the starter homes for an entire generation. About 15 years ago, we began to see many luxury townhomes being built in prime areas, beginning in the range of $1 million or more; and prices continue to rise. I recently read that the 60-story Woolworth Building in Manhattan will soon be converted to ultraluxury condominiums. Prices haven't been set, but estimates run in the range of $6 million to $12 million per suite. Obviously, these prices are far out of the range of a typical beginning family. Again, things change.

Still, many townhomes are available, accessible, and affordable for the nation's families. America has always been a country dedicated to freedom. Certainly the freedom to own property and capitalize on the appreciation of real estate has had a dramatic and positive impact on the growth of our economy, our nation, and our people. I don't see that changing.

A SHARE IN OWNERSHIP

The cooperative, or co-op, has always been a different sort of creature. As previously noted, buyers purchase stock in a corporation that is managed by a board of directors, which has the power to accept or reject new shareholders—new neighbors. It's just like owning shares in a major corporation; in fact, co-ops are privately held corporations. You own your shares and can keep them or sell them at your discretion, provided there is a buyer.

Co-ops were set up primarily to provide owners of the corporation—the neighbors—a measure of real control over who would and who would not be allowed to become a member of these small communities. Someone who belongs to a minority group, who has a lifestyle different from the majority of owners, or who is somehow different enough in another way could easily find himself or herself blackballed and unable to purchase shares in a residential unit within a co-op building.

The results of such policies should be obvious. Many famous, and many more not so well-known people, including celebrities, were rejected by co-ops simply because they were African American or Jewish or whatever. These were people who had the necessary income and were often admired, and even loved, by millions of people throughout the country. Yet they were still blackballed.

I came across a news article about this situation not too long ago. The Washington, D.C., Office of Human Rights found probable cause that a co-op within the district had refused to sell shares to a man because he was gay and had an African American roommate. The case has been sent to the city's Commission on Human Rights because co-ops have the right to discriminate against individuals or families but not on the basis of race or sexual orientation.

According to the prospective buyer, he had planned on using profits from the sale of a property he owned for the down payment, his bank had approved him for a loan, and the co-op's finance committee had given the green light to his application. The prospective buyer claimed the board of directors rejected the application because it didn't want a mixed-race gay couple in the building. Representatives of the co-op denied the charges, noting that gays and blacks had been, and still were, living in the co-op and claiming the rejection was due instead to certain tax matters related to the purchase.

The Office of Human Rights found probable cause that the rejection of the application on the tax basis was merely an excuse to cover a case of sexual orientation and racial discrimination. Things then got even more interesting. The couple that had planned on selling their shares to the mixed-race gay couple filed their own lawsuit against the co-op, claiming economic loss as a result of the rejected application. Discrimination often has a negative impact beyond the individuals against whom the discrimination is directed. The Office of Human Rights found probable cause in the seller's case as well. As of this writing, the case is apparently still on appeal and indicates how complex the ownership situation can become.

We don't find too many new co-ops being constructed these days. But there are still many existing co-ops adhering to rules allowing shareholders and/or boards of directors to determine who may and who may not buy into the company. I've learned a few lessons the hard way about co-ops myself.

In 1993 an attorney contacted me to auction a co-op apartment in one of Chicago's finest neighborhoods. The shareholder had relocated out of state and had a 3,000-square-foot, 14th-floor unit overlooking the lake and one of the city's finest parks—a beautiful location and a great buy. During the marketing period, raw power asserted itself. A neighbor was a member of one of Chicago's most prominent families and an heir to a vast fortune. I was contacted by the next door neighbor and told in no uncertain terms that the neighbor would be the only buyer qualified to acquire the apartment.

Wow! I asked why and was told by the next door neighbor quite bluntly that the neighbor owned the unit next door, wanted to make the purchase to expand the size of his home, and as a leader on the co-op's board of directors would never allow anyone other than himself to purchase the unit. Talk about raw power. That was a big lesson for yours truly. They say "you can't fight city hall," but it's equally true that you can't fight a determined co-op board of directors.

I'm not knocking all co-ops. Provided discrimination is within the law it can be a very positive thing. I'd discriminate against a drug dealer trying to buy into my co-op. Wouldn't you? If such a restrictive housing situation appeals to you, then the purchase of shares in a co-op is certainly worth investigation. Please note that financing for a co-op does not involve a conventional mortgage.

I'm Here to Say They're Here to Stay

Regardless of your opinions of minorities, they're here to stay, and they will continue to claim larger shares of the American dream. According to a 2003 article by the National Association of Realtors, <REALTOR .org>, more than 40 percent of net new homeowners during the past five years were minorities; of the six million net new households during the past five years, more than one-half were headed by minorities; during the next 20 years, a rise of 15.3 million minority households can be expected; by 2020, 25 percent of all homeowners will be minorities; by 2020, the number of minority homeowners will increase from 10.4 million to 22.5 million.[2]

There's an important fact to remember about American history. Whatever your background, at some point your ancestors were immigrants and members of a minority.

These days, the most popular entry for people into the housing market is through a condominium. The price tag on a single-family dwelling in an urban area has just skyrocketed out of reach of most first-time buyers. These are no longer the days of your grandparents. Neither are they the low-cost days of the hippy era. Take heart. As I noted earlier, purchasing a condo isn't settling for second best or a lesser option. Condos are more popular than ever before and that popularity continues to rise. Affordability is just one of the reasons.

SAY AMEN TO AMENITIES

It's summer, a hot summer Saturday afternoon. You're sitting in the shade in the backyard of your single-family dwelling while enjoying a cold glass of lemonade, ice tea, or your favorite adult beverage. Life is good. Then you notice that the grass has grown a little too high. The flower bed needs weeding and leaves are choking your rain gutters. Well, there goes the pleasant afternoon. It's time to break out the lawn mower, the garden hoe, the ladder, and other tools. You'll probably be breaking out a lot of sweat, too.

Let's move on to winter, a cold winter Saturday afternoon. You're sitting all toasty warm in front of a roaring television set sipping hot cocoa, hot tea, or your favorite adult beverage. Life is good. Then you notice that the snow has covered your walkway. Ice has accumulated on your steps, and an icy breeze is slipping under the front door. It's time to break out the snow shovel, the rock salt, and the weather stripping and say goodbye to that ball game you wanted to watch.

One of the benefits of living in association housing is being able to avoid most or all of the above chores and more. Whether you choose a townhome, a condo, or a co-op, the amenities that are automatically yours can help you maintain a lifestyle that will be the envy of your rake-, hoe-, and shovel-toting, single-family-dwelling-owning friends and associates.

When you join an association, part of your financial responsibility is a monthly association fee or assessment. You'll find that most associations have already hired at least one maintenance man, a landscaping company, and many other professionals to care for not only the jointly owned amenities such as stairwells, hallways, and sidewalks but also for the living areas of the association's members. Sometimes a doorman is even part of the deal. All that personal service leaves a lot of time for sipping lemonade and watching ball games.

There's a price to pay and you will pay it, but there's also a price to pay when you have the responsibility for keeping up a single-family dwelling. There are the hard costs of tools and upkeep, but there's also a very real cost of your own labor and the time that labor drains from your other activities. Many people find the trade-off in association living well worth the price tag; I think most of them feel they're coming out way ahead. You develop an ongoing pride of ownership in a property in tip-top shape without your hands getting dirty.

In some smaller associations, usually in buildings with eight or fewer units, members (or a member) may take it upon themselves to service the property. No, you probably won't see your next-door neighbor don a starched uniform and start opening the association's front door for you, but you just might see him or her landscaping the common ground, shoveling snow off the sidewalks, putting out salt to melt the ice on the sidewalks and steps, weeding the flower beds, installing a window screen, replacing a washer, and being the general fix-it person for the association. Sometimes the fix-it person gets paid for the work, but more often the person doesn't. Regardless of how many individuals or companies are involved, the real draw for many people is the simple fact that someone else has the responsibility for doing the chores. The appearance of the property will always be maintained and needed repairs made.

Naturally, the amount of amenities available varies according to the property you choose. A starter-home condominium will have fewer amenities than an ultraluxury condo. Sometimes an amenity can be in the form of heat included in your assessment. In other cases, your amenities can be quite a bit more. As a potential homeowner, it's important that you understand precisely what amenities will be available to you. They may be a list of basic items, such as parking. But will you get access to a parking garage, covered parking, or just a slot on the open concrete? Who is responsible for painting the interior of your unit? How quickly can maintenance workers respond to an emergency? Are there plans to add to, or delete, the list of amenities?

As you move up the economic ladder, more amenities will be available. Many associations have access to a health club, a spa, and other luxuries. If your unit is part of a hotel complex, you might even be able to dial room service. A simple phone call could bring polite service personnel to your front door with a bucket of ice, a hot pizza from the kitchen, or a tray of your favorite beverages. Believe me, that isn't bad. It isn't bad at all.

The point of this section is to let you know that amenities are normal, customary, and available to you as a homeowner in association housing. When conducting your initial research, be sure to ask your Realtor for a list of all the amenities in the associations you are considering. Townhome association amenities in condominiums and co-ops may be very similar but may also vary considerably. In recent years many developers have created mixed communities that include both condos and townhomes and are often centered on a park or a golf course. By being a member of a larger association, you may have access to additional amenities whether you're living in one of the condos or one of the townhomes. These amenities could include:

- A golf course
- A "19th hole"
- The clubhouse
- Tennis courts
- Swimming pool
- Barbecue areas

- A spa
- Jogging or bicycle tracks
- Mature trails
- Park areas

Amenities offered by association living provide convenience, pleasure, comfort, pride of ownership, and peace of mind. When compared with the labor involved in maintaining a single-family dwelling, many people look to a condo, a co-op, or a townhome, sign on the dotted line, and shout "Amen!"

MANY CONVENIENCES, MINIHEADACHES

Home ownership is a major element of the American dream, but the benefits come with a lot of headaches. Membership in an association can turn benefits into miniheadaches or, in many cases, eliminate most of them altogether. The association is a great resource when your property needs maintenance or repair. You may need a plumbing fixture replaced, a room painted, a crack in the ceiling or a broken window repaired, or any number of problems handled. Instead of getting your hands dirty, scraping your knuckles, bumping your head, and using up your list of curses, as a member of the association all you have to do is make a phone call and wait for the plumber, electrician, carpenter, landscaper, or other professional in the form of maintenance personnel to show up and take care of the problem.

In addition, it's nice to have professionals on hand who have some history with your building, people who know the customs and traditions of the property and the people living there. Because the association represents such a large amount of work (and profit), it commands far greater loyalty and response than any individual—a huge plus when the city is bogged down in an ice storm and virtually everyone in town is screaming for service. Who's going to get the fastest response: the lone homeowner in the suburbs or the 500-member association down the street? You do the math. Having that kind of convenience at hand sure beats flipping through the Yellow Pages and then trying to cajole a series of tradespeople to put you at the top of their lists.

Location and proximity to work is another convenience. The boom in condominium development near downtown areas in the past ten years is due in large part to the desire of people to live near their work-place. An associate of mine lives in Houston and has a wonderful family and a good job with an international corporation. She and her family live in a bedroom community a considerable distance from her office in the core of the city. Every workday she gets up at 4 AM so she can arrive at the park-and-ride at 6 AM and arrive at work by 8 AM. After work she rushes to get to the park-and-ride by 6 PM so she can be home by 8 PM to spend a few moments with her family before she goes to bed at 9 PM to be rested by the 4 AM wake-up call. When her kids were very young, they were often asleep by the time she got home so that often she didn't really get to spend any quality time with her children during the week. That's a pretty big sacrifice for any family. All that we really have to enjoy in life is time, and only so much of it is allotted to each of us. By living closer to work, we can invest time with our families, our interests, and our passions rather than spending time in traffic jams.

The housing boom in the city has had other positive effects. Retail-ers follow their customers, and the move back to town has encouraged many grocery chains, health clubs, movie theaters, medical profession-als, and other providers of goods and services to make the move, too. Twenty or 30 years ago this move to town would have been unheard of, and anyone making such a prediction would have been considered something of a kook. But even in the country's rust belt, where people have for years abandoned commercial property, we are seeing serious redevelopment.

This redevelopment is in the form of adaptive reuse. Loft buildings and Class C office buildings are being converted into more profitable residential association housing or being combined into innovative mixed-use reuse projects with retail stores on the lower levels. Such a dramatic change has fostered the development of prime residential neighborhoods in previously underused or abandoned property.

A major factor in the growth and renaissance of many downtown areas is the return of the baby boomers. Many of the families who moved to the suburbs in the sixties, seventies, and eighties have raised their children. They're moving into or toward retirement and are look-ing to improve the quality of their life. Many of them are selling their traditional single-family dwellings to buy nice condominiums in adap-tive reuse loft buildings and in newer buildings on the outskirts of down-town areas. Who would have thought that "old mom 'n dad" would sell that split-level ranch in the suburbs and move downtown to be as cool as their kids? Things tend to come full circle. Young folks just beginning their families purchase a small condominium, a co-op, or a townhome as a starter home. Now, older families are looking at the same investments so that they can enjoy the investment values, the amenities, and the convenience of association living.

The bottom line: For an ever-growing number of individuals and families, townhomes, condominiums, and co-operatives are the best option for claiming their share of the American dream.

2

NEW OR PREOWNED PROPERTY?

Part One

*"The way to get ahead is to start now. If you start now,
you will know a lot next year that you don't know now and that
you would not have known next year if you had waited."*

William Feather

That's right, start now: Even if you can't make the payments at your current income level; even if you don't have a down payment; and even if you think home ownership is an option only next year or the year after. Start now. I cannot overemphasize the importance of doing your homework before purchasing a townhome, condo, or co-op. For most folks the purchase of a home is the single most important financial move they'll ever make. It is essential that you research every aspect of this purchase long before you write that deposit check. Richard Cushing said, "Plan ahead: It wasn't raining when Noah built the ark."

This book will help you plan ahead. You're about to make the biggest purchase of your life. Together, we'll make sure that it will be a safe, sound, and secure investment. Trust me. Every moment you invest in researching your new home will be paid back by years of satisfaction, joy, and pride of ownership.

Buying a home is always exciting, but there are few things on Earth that can match the excitement of buying that first home. Fortunately, there's been a lot of building during the past two decades, so there are a lot of homes to be bought. During the new economy of the 1990s, everyone in real estate was working. Construction was at an all-time high, and the prices of association living dwellings were accelerating every day.

Times were so good that people were buying contracts on unbuilt properties and selling them by the time construction was complete. Prices were rising so fast that the owners could receive a substantial profit before they even moved in. Economies rise and fall. Sometimes it's a buyer's market and sometimes sellers call the shots. Regardless of the market, when you decide to purchase a townhome, condo, or co-op, you'll need to cover a lot of different bases to make sure you're getting the most for your money, the wisest investment for your future, and the best environment for your lifestyle.

When you buy a newly constructed home, you have a wide variety of options not available when you buy a resale. This alone is enough to move some buyers from the buy-resale frame of mind over to the buy-new mindset. For example, when you buy a new condominium, co-op, or townhome, you're able to make choices that may include paint colors, bathroom and other fixtures, tile, carpeting, kitchen countertops, lighting fixtures, appliances, cabinet pulls, door knobs, and just about anything you can imagine. The quality and number of these choices quite naturally vary according to the price of the unit. Ultraluxury units have more options than luxury units, which in turn have more options than starter units.

Pricing for starter units in urban areas varies from market to market, but figures below $250,000 are common. Even in new starter units, you still have a number of choices. That customization of your own home begins a long and satisfying experience called "pride of ownership."

EXAMINE THE WARRANTY

A warranty is a guarantee that the physical condition of your property and the common elements of the association are sound. They're issued on new construction or new conversions throughout the country and are usually for a period of one year. If something breaks down, cracks, leaks, or is in need of maintenance or repair during the warranty period, the builder, the general contractor, or the appropriate subcontractor will make repairs at his or her expense. Warranties aren't offered on resales.

A warranty is only as good as the person or company issuing it. The first and foremost element of any warranty you examine should be the reputation of the people standing behind it. How far back are they standing? For example, if your roof springs a leak, a lazy, inefficient, or dishonest contractor will show up in his or her own good time—if at all. A lifetime warranty from such a person isn't worth the paper it's fabricated on. Part of your homework is to research the reputation in your community of the association and the people and companies providing warranties for that property. You're going to be living there for some time, and you don't want to be subjected to an unnecessary and constant drip-drip-drip from the ceiling into your morning coffee.

I'm a developer, and I take my warranty responsibilities very seriously. It's not that I'm the "last of the good guys." I'm a good businessman and that means operating under a strict code of ethics, taking care of my customers, and building the best reputation in the community I can. I develop vintage buildings in Chicago, sometimes making modest renovations and sometimes gutting the structure to start from scratch. Whatever type of project I take on, I know my reputation will be based on how professionally I handle it. One of the worst things that could happen would be for the Realtors in Chicago to boycott my projects because they know I won't honor my warranties. I never want that to happen—and it never will.

For ethical, and also for very practical, reasons, my company's policy is to honor my warranties. If reasonable requests are made, we even honor expired warranties of the original developer. If you're interested in such projects in the Chicago area, please look me up. If you're in another part of the country, please find individuals and companies that conduct their business in a similar manner. It's worth the effort to find us.

Look for associations, developers, and contractors with outstanding reputations. Why should you settle for anything less? Read your local newspapers, especially the business and real estate columns. Learn which developers consistently create a quality product and which ones are consistently being sued, called back to repair shoddy work, or receive a lot of bad press. Also listen to the word on the street. If you know anyone in the construction trades, ask for a confidential opinion of different developers. You might be surprised at how many builders with supposedly solid reputations produce less-than-satisfactory work.

There is much more to enjoying your home than basking in the broad smile of a salesperson's face. For example, you want to make sure that the plumbing works in the unit above your living space. If a leak develops, you'll want to know that the drip-drip-drip will be addressed before your ceiling is stained, your carpet smudged, and your morning coffee has a certain ceiling/floor tile "whang." In this and similar circumstances, you're obviously encountering an insurance claim situation, but the work to repair the problem should still be in the hands of the contractor. You want to make sure those are capable hands.

Any warranty should have teeth to it. There are important considerations when choosing between a new or preowned townhome, condo, or co-op. In most cases the developers and contractors will be men, women, and companies that have been in business long enough to build sound reputations. Still, check them out.

EXAMINE THE FINANCIAL RESERVES

Another factor that many association buyers don't consider is a major one. An association developer should have the financial reserves on hand to bear the cost of repair and renovation of new construction. Make sure your developer has deep pockets and has not only the capacity to do your work but the capacity to do it when you need it. Ask for and check out your developer's references. Examine the projects the developer has done over the years, and remember the old adage, "Beauty is only skin deep, but ugly runs all the way to the bone." Don't be fooled by a beautiful or imposing structure. Ask tenants, neighbors, construction people, and Realtors about the soundness of that structure. Have there been many complaints? What types of complaints? Were problems resolved quickly or were there delays and hassles? Here is a list of ten questions you should ask previous buyers.

1. Did you receive delivery of your unit on the date you were promised?
2. Was the unit complete when you did your walk-through prior to closing?
3. Did the developer complete the punch-list items listed at that final walk-through promptly and within the agreed time frame?

4. Were there any problems present after closing and did the developer attend to them promptly?
5. Was the turnover of the condominium association smooth and thorough to the owners?
6. Were the projected assessments accurate, or were they less than they should have been?
7. Was the developer attentive to your questions, and did he or she return calls promptly?
8. Would you buy another home from this developer in the future?
9. Was the developer helpful in giving your lender the property report and condominium questionnaire in a timely manner?
10. Were there any unexpected items that showed up at closing?

Use these questions as a basis for your own list. Your developer should be proud to give you a list of customer names and phone numbers. Ask for at least three names in three different properties.

EXAMINE THE MUNICIPALITY

Some municipalities hold developers to strict account for adhering to their warranties. Others are more lax, and still others have tough regulations that are pretty much ignored. The attitude of the community and "city fathers" toward the matter of warranties should be a particular concern to anyone entering into association housing.

The village of Evanston, one of Chicago's northern suburbs, provides a good example. A builder or developer has to escrow a percentage of the sales proceeds of every condominium unit within the city to guarantee that a reserve is available after closing. Evanston goes a step further and requires that a certain percentage be retained by the city in an escrow account to assure that a developer actually has the money to repair and maintain warranty items after closing. Essentially, the developer's money is held hostage to make sure the developer lives up to his or her end of the bargain. The developer cannot get the money back until the warranty has expired and the developer has met his or her obligations to the new owners. The relevant section of the Evanston City Code is printed in Appendix A.

Obviously, Evanston's requirements were put in place because someone, sometime, somewhere experienced warranty problems. It's a good idea to check in your community or the community to which you want to move to see what rules and regulations are in place to protect homebuyers. I imagine most communities are lacking in this area, but even knowing that is valuable because it let's you know that you have to take even more personal responsibility for your purchase.

EXAMINE YOUR OPTIONS

You often have the option at closing of buying a warranty covering your mechanical systems and appliances. Sometimes such a warranty is provided by the developer, but more often you'll have to acquire it yourself through the developer or the Realtor or on your own. Such warranties act as an insurance policy for the protected items.

Home Warranty of America <www.servicemaster.com> is one such company that provides these warranties. The type of warranty it and others offer has two important basics. First, it protects the developer if problems develop in used mechanical systems and appliances; second, it provides the buyer peace of mind.

A friend of mine was saved a small fortune by Home Warranty of America. He bought a preowned house in the early nineties but within only a few months began smelling gas from a defective line. The wall between his kitchen and family room had to be removed, new gas piping installed, and then the wall rebuilt. Except for the deductible, the entire expense was covered by the warranty.

As I write this book, the cost of this type of warranty is about $450 or less. Items covered under such a warranty could include the heating unit, air conditioning unit, refrigerator, stove, microwave, washer/ dryer, and many other electrical and/or gas appliances. That $450 is an amazingly small figure compared with the amount of money you could pay to cover any number of small problems, big hassles, or major disasters.

EXAMINE THE SALES REPORT

If you're moving into a new association housing development, you'll want to know how the developer's sales are going. Are there a lot of excited buyers? Are sales moving along or just barely moving along?

Are there any sales at all? You probably don't want to be the only one or one of the few families living in a community that lacks, well, the rest of the community.

During the eighties the country experienced a tremendous boom in housing, a boom that nearly went bust when President Reagan signed the Tax Reform Act of 1986. Reaction took a few years, but between 1989 and 1994, events pulled the rug out from under the industry. The Resolution Trust Corporation (RTC) was formed to liquidate troubled banks and savings and loans, as well as their real estate holdings.

Prior to 1986, financial institutions could lend money to developers under limited restrictions, a bandwagon many individuals, investors, and companies jumped on. But some of them took too long a leap. Remember a key rule of life: things change, and the financial picture changed during those years. Many financial institutions overextended themselves. During the financial frenzy, some institutions made questionable loans to people and organizations unable to repay them. Banks and S&Ls ran out of money and could no longer fulfill their lending requirements to legitimate developers. To make matters worse, the country entered a mild recession, which further restricted the flow of money.

Our company represented a Denver savings and loan corporation that had made a loan to help develop homes in Lincoln Park, a prominent Chicago neighborhood. Seventeen units went unsold, but a couple of families had moved into two of the units. These poor folks were essentially stranded for two years during the foreclosure proceedings, in which the lender was waiting to take back the 17 unsold units. For two years no assessments were paid, the developer was gone, and an out-of-state bank was trying to manage the property long distance. Worse than that, the entire development was in various stages of disarray and disrepair. Necessary warranty work was ignored and maintenance neglected as were landscaping and other important matters; and there weren't even any neighbors with whom to share their grief. This wasn't exactly the environment those two families signed on for when they moved into their new homes. Eventually, the bank sold the property to a developer who finished the job, but I can guarantee that was a long and unpleasant two-year stretch for the two original families.

I see this kind of thing all the time. Developers start out with the best of intentions, but financing dries up, the economy turns sour, someone makes a series of costly mistakes in management, or expenses take a dramatic rise. They find themselves out of capital and unable to acquire more funds, and development grinds to a halt. Be extra careful when considering a new development or one under construction. Find out how many units have already been sold and how many contracts are on the table. Make sure you have the ability to step away from, or bail out of, a contract if your developer becomes incapable of completing the project.

I saw the same kind of problem arise for a bunch of empty nesters in Buffalo Grove, a city northwest of Chicago. It was a planned unit development (PUD) called Town Place and Town Center and was one of the first developments I acquired. The PUD was to have a shopping center, 150 townhomes, and 88 condominiums plus the normal amenities. Unfortunately, the developer couldn't finish the project, so phase two turned into a group of unfinished townhomes, incomplete condos, and undeveloped land. The property went back to the bank, but the bank was shut down by the government. I jumped in to buy the condos and townhomes, finished them, and sold the land to a developer who would complete the PUD. Things worked out, but those poor empty nesters must have felt that they were living in a ghost town.

EXAMINE EVERYTHING ELSE

The risks versus the rewards for buying a new condo, co-op, or townhome seem about equal on the balance scale. Review all the condominium and association documents and make sure your attorney reads them too. Be aware of all your obligations and the obligations of the developer and the association. Leave no gray area unexamined. Larger developments are often built in phases, so it's important to know (1) in which phase you're buying, (2) the schedule for phases two and three, and (3) how sales and construction are going.

Larger complexes often have such amenities as a swimming pool, health club, golf course, tennis courts, parks, and other common areas for the enjoyment of the tenants. It's not unusual for these amenities to be last on the completion list. If golf (or tennis or swimming) is one of the reasons you've chosen that community, then you don't want to wait an unnecessarily long time to enjoy that activity. Again, ask around and get solid information regarding the reputation of your developer. It's worth it for your peace of mind alone.

You will probably be required to provide the association a deposit equal to twice your monthly assessment, the funds that create the initial reserves necessary to operate the association. For example, if your monthly assessment is $250, your deposit will be twice that amount—$500—plus your prorated assessment for that month.

It's the developer's responsibility to begin paying assessments for all of the unsold units from the day of the closing of the first unit. For example, if you're paying a $250 per month assessment for your unit, the developer should be paying $250 per unit for all of the unsold units. Assessments are based on a percentage of ownership, and as a rule that figure is determined by the sales price per unit rather than the amount of square feet within it. In other words, if you own one unit out of ten, you won't necessarily be responsible for 10 percent of the square footage. The amount will vary according to your percentage of ownership.

Rules and regulations vary state to state, county to county, and city to city, but most of your questions can be answered by taking a close look at the declarations of the new association. In Chicago, a property report must be issued by the developer for any buildings with seven or more units. The report must contain the following items:

- The engineering report
- The price list
- The condominium survey
- The list of building code violations, if any
- The warranty
- The sales brochure
- The names of the developer, architect, accountant, sales agents, etc.
- Any and all disclosures

Condominium declarations explain the rules governing living in the association. They cover such areas as whether pets are allowed; how to display a For Sale sign on the building; signage restrictions and allowances; locations of satellite dishes; swimming pool hours; parking requirements; and any number of other lifestyle considerations. Naturally, these declarations not only vary from state to state or city to city but also from building to building. Still, wherever you are there will be a property report containing condominium declarations you can access. Please see that you do. Declarations can be amended, but you have to follow a process and record any changes with your local title company.

An important part of the property report is the engineer's report, which tells you a lot about what the builder did and did not do during construction. It lists the architect, the accountant, the Realtor, the builder, the developer, and the various trades represented by general contractors and subcontractors. Also included is a list of warranties that are passed on to the association. You certainly want to make sure that you receive all applicable warranties and warranty papers the builder possesses. You also want a copy of the original blueprints and building plans in case you have problems down the road.

A good example of what can happen down the road involved Water Tower Place along Chicago's Magnificent Mile (North Michigan Avenue). The development included a condominium complex above a vertical mall, the brainchild of Philip Klutznick, who had served as President Jimmy Carter's secretary of commerce in 1980 and 1981. This building was a first for Chicago, the first shopping mall with a hotel above it and a luxury condominium complex above that. The development attracted a lot of Chicago's rich and famous, including television host and celebrity Oprah Winfrey. Years later Donald Trump copied this concept with his Trump Tower in New York City.

In 2000, almost a quarter of a century after the construction of Water Tower Place, the plumbing risers supplying water to more than 200 units needed a significant amount of repair. (Risers are the pipes bringing water up to the apartments.) Every wall and every common area in every tier had to be opened up, and the risers had to be replaced inch by inch, a process that took four years to complete. The owners were charged a special assessment to help cover the additional expense; in addition, sales of the units were deterred because of all the construction. My key point: Nearly 25 years after the building was completed, the original blueprints and plans were essential elements in keeping the building in good working condition. The same problem could arise even in a small building, so it is important that you have a solid and in-depth knowledge of your condo, co-op, or townhome and its environment. You'll never know when you'll need it.

MONITOR YOUR DELIVERY DATE

Before taking possession of a new home, you certainly want to use the services of a home inspector or at least someone with a depth of industry knowledge. Make sure that everything you think should be in place *is* in place and in good working order. If things aren't shipshape, you'll want someone who is capable of recognizing the problem(s) and of recommending corrective measures.

Development contracts have a specific completion date, the time when you should be able to move in and begin the good life on Easy Street. Delays are uncommon, but they can happen.

ANTICIPATE THE FUTURE

In addition to knowing what your developer and your association have planned for the future, you should also investigate what the owners and developers of nearby properties have in mind. For example, you might have a great view of the park over the top of a small business just beneath your window. What happens to your view if that property is torn down and replaced by a high-rise office building or apartment complex? If the view is a significant factor in your decision, make time to explore what that view will be next year or even many years down the road.

My wife and I lived in a condominium on the 28th floor of a building on Chicago's Magnificent Mile. It was a corner apartment with a beautiful view of Lake Michigan and Lakeshore Drive. Shortly after we were married, a developer bought the property right across from our condo and began construction on a development called One Magnificent Mile. Not only did we endure several years of construction, but every day we watched our beautiful view disappear inch by inch. Soon our view to the north was of the apartments across the way. During the time all of this was going on, another development called the Bloomingdale's Building began blocking our view to the south.

Every down has an up. Although we lost our views, the value of our property tripled. So what's the bottom line? Make sure of the reasons motivating you to buy an apartment. If a view is a strong motivator, then make sure someone else isn't planning to build something between you and the scenery.

PARKING

City codes require that most new developments provide parking. Townhomes usually have a garage next to or beneath the structure. Condo and co-op owners may have access to a parking garage, covered parking, or an open parking lot, and these spaces may be available for purchase or by rental. Parking is certainly an aspect of association living you'll want to check out in advance.

If you can buy your parking space, do so. Lock it in. Even better, buy two spaces if possible. It's a nice courtesy for any guests you may have, but more than that, an extra space adds a lot of resale value to your unit. The extra cost is more than offset by enhanced value and salability.

You can even rent the extra space to a neighbor and turn it into a profit-making venture. Water Tower Place, mentioned earlier in this chapter, is a prime example. The developer acquired ownership of the parking garage and leased spaces to the condominium tenants. That property has been creating millions in revenue since the seventies. If you were to purchase a condo unit in Water Tower, your parking would be limited to the situation inherited from the previous owner. Again, check out each aspect of your purchase. Assume nothing and ask a lot of specific questions.

MAINTENANCE ON
NEW CONSTRUCTION

Native Americans have a saying that "only the rocks live forever." Everything else has a finite lifetime. That includes plumbing, electrical wiring, wall paint, flooring, ceilings, roofing tiles, sidewalks, tennis courts, swimming pools, and golf courses. Maintenance and repair are major ongoing responsibilities. As a prospective owner, it's your responsibility to make sure those bases are covered.

Before you sign any dotted line, find out which individuals or which companies are responsible for maintenance and repair of your unit and its environs. Is there only a janitor who doubles as a handyman? Is there a team on duty? Is there a list of professionals to call for immediate response to an emergency? Who does what in terms of day-to-day maintenance, repair, and upkeep? Be sure to investigate the reputation of anyone or any company with these responsibilities. Just as with a warranty, maintenance is only as reliable as the people who provide the service.

Well, as William Feather promised at the beginning of this chapter, you now know a lot more than you did when you began. There's a lot more to learn about the pros and cons of owning new versus preowned property. Let's see how much more knowledge you can pick up in Chapter 3.

3

NEW OR PREOWNED PROPERTY?

Part Two

*"All the problems of the world could be settled easily
if men were only willing to think."*

Nicholas Murray Butler

PROS AND CONS OF PREOWNED PROPERTIES

All the problems of buying association property could be settled easily if buyers were only willing to think. Throughout my real estate career I've been continually amazed by the number of people who make the biggest purchases of their life without really thinking through the decision. As a soon-to-be homeowner, you must accept the responsibility to make sure you're buying a safe, sound, and secure home that will enhance your lifestyle for many years to come.

Most property sold in this country has been owned by someone else. Statistically, 20 percent of the population moves every year; that's one of every five Americans selling and buying homes and means a terrific turnover of homes every year, many of which are condos, co-ops, and townhomes. The motivations for the turnover are numerous, but the chief one is a change in occupation. People today are very mobile, more so than ever in our history. The rapidly expanding, ever-shifting global economy dictates it. The era of going to work for "the company" for life, even for generations, is over. For most of us, that seemingly unsettling thought isn't really unsettling at all. It means we're free agents and can move wherever the opportunity shouts "Over here!" That leaves a lot of very good, very affordable, very attainable houses on the market.

Most people buy an existing home because they are generally more affordable than new construction; units under $250,000 are a good entry level for this market. Another big factor in the popularity of existing homes is a guaranteed move-in date. New construction can be held up by weather problems, delays in delivery of materials, labor strikes, or any number of other sound reasons. The move-in date can become a constantly shifting "X" on a calendar, whereas existing property . . . exists. You can agree on a date, and the dwelling is there waiting for you.

LOOK BEFORE YOU REAP

"You reap what you sow" is more than just an adage. It's a fact of life. Before you reap the benefits of association living, you should make sure you're not leaping into a financial nightmare. Of course, you'll want to do a walk-through of the property to get a sense of space and how well you and your family will fit in. If you're moving into a building with six or more units, you'll certainly want to take a close look at the original property report to discover what was and what was not completed by the original developer. High on the list of a number of other areas worth looking into are special assessments and disclosures.

Special assessments aren't called *special* because they're considered treats for the homeowner. As the buyer of a preowned unit, you won't be required to put up the amount of the first two months (or more) of the monthly assessment to help set up the reserve account. Nonetheless, you will be required to pay an assessment or maintenance fee. You should make yourself aware of these figures before you make the purchase.

You may think that you're getting off easy by not having to pay two times the assessment for the original reserve, but keep an eye out for the words *special assessment*. Associations use them to cover unexpected expenses that can't be covered by the reserve account. In other words, if a meteor hits the roof and there's not enough money in the pot for repairs, the association taps the owners. Whatever the maintenance or repair item may be, you and the other owners will find that you have an obligation to pay a special assessment to cover the costs. When that happens, it's possible that the cause of the assessment was known all along to the association, and the repairs are being deferred to a later time. In this situation you should have something in writing from the owner of the property that protects you from such a special assessment coming immediately after you make the purchase.

It is for this reason that you want disclosures from the previous owner about any problems or potential problems with the property. Some disclosures are required by law; for example, federal law requires a lead paint disclosure on any home built before 1978 because lead paint, which was commonly used before 1978, has certain health risks. The seller and/or Realtor will provide this disclosure as well as a pamphlet titled *Hazards of Lead Paint in Your Home.*

Different states have different disclosure requirements. Generally, the disclosures make you aware of material defects in plumbing, electrical, environmental, or other systems. The document should be signed by the seller and dated, and you'll sign and date it to signify your approval. You also have the right to have your own inspector examine the property. Disclosures are critical. If you don't receive all the information you are due, later on you could invest a lot of money in maintenance and repair to take care of problems that were actually the responsibility of the previous owner. As always, "Let the buyer beware," so make sure you get every bit of information possible before making a commitment.

Get to know your future neighbors too. As you're touring prospective properties, consider the community as well as the condo. Visit the areas on the weekend, when lots of people are at home, on the streets, and in the parks. Do you like what you see, or do you spot a potential problem that needs investigation? You won't be living in a vacuum, so be sure you'll be comfortable in your new environment.

Recently, I was working out at my health club with a fellow Realtor. When I asked about the tired look in his eyes, he said that he lived next to some senior citizens in his townhome association. Because the walls are thin, noises from the seniors' home had kept him up all night. I smiled and was about to use the old phrase, "There may be snow on the roof, but there's fire in the furnace," when he smiled and shook his head. The seniors weren't making the noise. It was their television set, which had been turned up to full volume so that the nearly deaf couple could hear their favorite shows.

I mention this because you want to be able to live comfortably in your new home. It's better to find out early about the noisy couple next door, the barking dog down the street, or the professional tuba player upstairs. Keep in mind that the neighbors will be checking you out too. Be sure to smile when you unload your bass drum.

Disclosures about pet restrictions are exceptionally important because so much emotion is tied to people's cats, dogs, parakeets, and boa constrictors. You don't want to find out that pets are prohibited the day you're moving your best friend into its new domicile. Not only should you review the disclosures, but you should ask the association president if there have been any amendments. Be sure to get a copy of any amendments. Also ask if any amendments are being proposed. "Pets allowed" could easily change to "No pets allowed" at the next association meeting.

Get all the information you can up front. Once you sign on, it's difficult to receive any kind of compensation for lack of disclosure. The attorney's fees, the legal and procedural hassles, and the time consumed make the process an unpleasant experience at best.

Of course, the most significant disclosure document is your contract. Everything should be spelled out in detail within that document, including the following:

- Price
- Personal property
- Amount of earnest money you're putting down
- Mortgage contingency clause
- Number of days allowed for attorney review
- Contingency clause for home inspection

Contracts are often just so much boilerplate, but you and your attorney should examine every detail nonetheless. Small variations from the norm could have huge consequences after you make your purchase.

TAKE ME TO YOUR LEADER

High on your list of priorities is a meeting with the leadership of your association. These folks can have a surprising amount of power over your lifestyle. You want to know what kind of people wield so much power and whether you can work with them. Leaders generally are very influential in decision making for the association. Like investing in a company or a mutual fund, you want to know the quality of management. You may even choose to become part of that management if your temperament, commitment, and drive so dictate.

One key item you want to check with the leadership, the seller, and your Realtor is the status of previous assessments. It's not unusual to buy a condo, co-op, or townhome from someone who is in arrears on his or her monthly assessment to the association. Sometimes a person can be seriously in arrears, and *you can inherit that debt.* It doesn't matter whether you created the debt; it can become yours the moment you sign the contract. Before you close and take title and obligation to the property, make certain that you get a signed paid assessment letter from the association president or treasurer stating that nothing is due to the association from the unit you are buying. You see, because the assessment is made to the unit, whoever owns it owes it. Such a liability can run into serious dollars and isn't the kind of "Welcome, neighbor" you want to experience. Fortunately, you can avoid such unpleasant surprises by asking questions, reading your disclosures, and requesting a paid assessment letter.

Protecting yourself, your family, and your investment up front is simple, easy, and relatively quick. Learning these lessons after making the purchase is comparable to what some people describe as "swimming in maple syrup." It's difficult, slow going, and always messy.

INSPECT YOUR INSPECTOR

Virtually every contract negotiation follows the same format. A property is put on the market for a price. A potential buyer makes a lower offer. The seller responds with a counteroffer, which is met with a counteroffer from the buyer, and so on and so on until a firm deal is struck. There are two conditions that you must—absolutely must—have in your contract. Fortunately, in most cases they are part of the boilerplate I mentioned, but if not, be sure to insert them. Insist on (1) enough time for your attorney to review the contract and (2) the right to conduct a home inspection.

The reason for number one is obvious. Purchasing property involves laws, ordinances, rules, and regulations requiring the attention of an expert in the field. The average layperson lacks the education and training to understand important details. More than that, laypeople just don't have time to stay current on the ever-changing nature of those laws, ordinances, rules, and regulations. Make time for your attorney and make sure that time is part of the contract.

The second condition needed in your contract is critical, because in a resale the warranty is not passed on to the new owner. Can you spot termite damage? Can you tell if the building is settling? Do you know how to recognize water damage? How are you at spotting electrical wiring problems? Do you know your way around a heating and cooling system? Have you considered the possible allergic reactions you might have to mold or mildew in the bathroom or in water-damaged Sheetrock that, on the surface, looks okay?

These items and many more can become a major drain on your income if major problems develop in the future. Think *Star Trek*. You need a real pro to scan the entire home for possible "hostiles."

Don't look in the phone book and hire just any old inspector. As in every other profession, there are winners, losers, and so-so performers. Get a winner. Ask around and do your homework. I have met inspectors who enjoy creating a sense of catastrophe with no real reason; some like to play games. Perhaps it's a power trip; I don't know, but I've seen some inspectors present completely benign items as problems. Again, let the buyer beware. Better yet, let the buyer get references.

DECISION TIME: WHICH IS THE BEST FOR YOU?

We live in a nation where options are commonplace, so common that we take for granted what most of the world's population would consider luxuries. Choice is a wonderful luxury, and as a homebuyer you are blessed with it.

If you've ever read my books or articles or attended my presentations and seminars, you know I recommend that you take a year to find your dream home. A year of research may seem like a long time, but it's nothing compared to the time you'll put into living in that dwelling. Get out in the community and make a list of possible purchases. Then start crossing off the ones that don't match your needs one at a time until you're left with the perfect selection.

Look inside as well as outside. Don't be fooled or overpowered by a beautiful exterior. Make sure the interior layout and design meet your living as well as your aesthetic needs—or can be adapted to them. And don't forget about the inspection. Believe me, an exterior means little if a worn-out pipe bursts and you find yourself bailing water out of the living room. Visualize how your furniture will look inside the new home. Will there be a good match or an awkward mismatch of styles and colors? Will you have to buy new furniture or renovate the interior? Where will the pets stay, and are pets even allowed?

It is critical for you to get out and look around—inside, outside, up, down, back, and forth. Any little thing you miss could turn out to be a major hassle later on. On rare occasions, homebuyers find the perfect property right off the bat. Do you know what usually happens? Because they've looked at so few houses, they're not confident in their feelings. They head out and look around some more only to find that their original favorite remains at the top of the list. Unfortunately, by the time they come to that realization, the property may have been sold to someone else. These are just some of the considerations you have to face.

I'd be the first to say that if you're trying to decide between new construction and a preowned property and both offer pretty much the same things at similar prices, you'd be foolish to pass the new home for the old. In that situation, buy the new one. With that caveat, you'll find most new buyers purchase preowned condos, co-ops, or townhomes. I've found this happens for two basic reasons: One is that resale homes are generally less expensive, a pretty good incentive; and, second, many older homes offer features that are no longer available in new or newer homes. If you've ever traveled east of the Mississippi, you will have noticed a large and well-maintained stock of vintage housing. Many of these older homes, especially the Victorian models, have architectural features that are just not cost effective for modern construction: high ceilings, pediments and articulated bay windows, thick walls with lots of soundproofing, arches, marble fireplace surrounds, and expensive finishes.

If you like that kind of lifestyle but don't want the hassles of an older home, don't give up. A lot of vintage housing has been renovated so that you can own modern conveniences without sacrificing the charm of bygone days. Even if the home hasn't been renovated, you could make changes on your own. You might be able to put in a new kitchen and modern bathroom features, build new closets, or alter the interior in any number of ways to make it more livable for you and your family.

Remember to check with your association before you get too far along with your renovations. It's likely that a long list of rules and regulations govern what types of renovations owners may and may not perform. In association housing, what one person does may have an impact on other owners. Renovation guidelines should be clearly stated in association bylaws. Always double-check to make certain there haven't been any changes or amendments you may have missed.

I recently sold a young man a unit in a vintage restoration. He wanted to make a fairly simple renovation, but he didn't take the trouble to check the appropriate rules. He opened up a wall to create more interior space. Nice for him, but a problem for the other owners on his tier, who lost the functioning of their doorbells and security buzzer systems as a result of his work. This was sloppy thinking on the young man's part as well as remarkably poor planning and a serious breech of neighborly courtesy. The poor fellow had to pay for all the damage he created and also had to invest a lot of personal time mending fences.

First-time homebuyers almost by definition have fewer choices when they purchase existing housing. That's just part of the deal and that's okay. Buying a preowned home is merely a first step, often the only one available to first-timers. It's a compromise but not a bad one. That's how most of us get started. It's a way to build equity and appreciation so you can trade up. Even so, you still have a lot of choices and options to explore.

Here is the way I got started. Before I became a real estate professional, I lived in a rental. At some point during the eighties, the light bulb in my head clicked on, and I realized that for a minimal down payment I could own a condo. I purchased a two-bedroom condo without parking in Chicago's Lakeview neighborhood for $68,000. I loved it. I loved the spaciousness, the elevated living room, large windows, high ceilings, built-in bookshelves, closet space, low assessments, a small second bedroom, a shared laundry, plenty of storage space in the basement, and even a small office subdivided from the original second bedroom. The only renovation I did was a bit of painting.

For a 30-year-old single male with a $7,000 down payment, this was a great way to move from renting to owning. The woman I married five years later also lived in a condo but with parking. That was a major issue at the time, so I sold my unit for $95,000 and moved in to her condo. Let's look at the math involved in those years.

My condo increased in value approximately 7 percent a year; this was when 10 percent interest was considered a great rate, so keep that in mind. My $7,000 investment earned 30 percent per year. Not bad. In addition, I deducted the interest and real estate taxes from my income taxes. All in all, the condo proved to be a terrific investment. In about five years, I earned $27,000, almost four times my original investment. Add to that the equity I had earned by paying down my mortgage for five years, and the total amount I walked away with was closer to $35,000.

We let that money rest in the bank until we were ready to put it to work. My wife and I decided to step up in the world, so we sold her condo. We used the equity on that property to buy a more substantial multiunit property and rented out the other two units, thereby realizing a nice cash flow for a number of years. Later, we refinanced that property, and as it appreciated in value we had a down payment to buy a lovely house in Chicago's Lincoln Park community.

Basically, you can do the same thing in the community of your choice. Ask around and you'll hear hundreds of similar stories. People all around you have continued, are continuing, and will continue to buy a small home, let it appreciate, and use their increased investment to buy a bigger and better house. *When you put your money to work for you, you don't have to work for your money.* This financial fact of life will happen to you in varying degrees when you purchase a home. Your capital appreciation and gains could be modest, but they could also be substantial depending on your location, the market, the economy, and numerous other factors.

People who have lived in the same property for an extended period will tell you that their real estate has appreciated at a much higher rate than they thought possible, and that is especially true during the past two or three decades.

Which option is best for you, new or preowned? Well, only you can say. But you should have your say only after conducting a year's worth of in-depth study and research. Property is generally a pretty sound investment. To borrow a phrase from Mark Twain, "They ain't making any more of it." New or preowned, it's your choice.

Make it a good one.

BUYING FOR LIVING

The best investment is the one you purchase to live in. Not only do you enjoy the comfort, security, and pride of ownership in your own home, but you also earn the advantages of a return on your investment and building equity. You can also enjoy a sort of tax shelter because you can use your mortgage interest and real estate taxes as a tax deduction. The money involved in owning a house isn't all outgo. I don't think you should allow investment considerations inordinate sway over your buying decisions. After all, you are going to *live* there, and you want a certain level of comfort and aesthetic value. Still, a home is an investment and should be examined in that light.

As an owner in association housing, you may not deduct your assessment for maintenance and upkeep of the common areas. A special assessment to improve the property and renovation expenses you incur will decrease the amount of capital gain you may have to pay when you eventually sell your unit. Again, home ownership in a condo, co-op, or townhome isn't a zero-sum game in which you constantly pay and pay and pay. There is balance because you build equity, enjoy tax advantages, and can reap a nice return on your investment when you sell to move up.

Over time, no favorable comparison can be made between renting and owning. A lot of folks wonder why they should assume the burden of a few more dollars a month just to have pride of ownership. That's shortsighted thinking, very shortsighted thinking. Rent money earns you a roof over your head for a month. That's it. The money you pay for home ownership is an investment that brings substantial returns. You're much better off in the long run as a homeowner.

I have accumulated many years of experience, and over the years I've come to the conclusion that, dollar for dollar, it costs the same to own a condo or townhome as it does to rent one. Remember, the rent money goes out and stays out. Your house payment goes out and then comes back in various profitable forms.

I attribute my observation on the inequality of rent versus ownership of condos to two factors. One, as interest rates decrease, property owners are able to borrow more money; more people therefore find condo and townhome living affordable and are moving from rentals to home ownership, which creates a lot of vacancies in the rental market.

Two, these days we're seeing more mortgage companies making 100 percent loans, which means loan institutions allow homebuyers to borrow all the money they need to make a purchase. Of course, borrowers must have good credit to get this type of loan.

America is a wonderful country for many reasons. Some of them are the insurance programs and guarantees to lenders in the form of private mortgage insurance programs that are designed to encourage home ownership. For example, there's private mortgage insurance (PMI) that provides default insurance to the loaner. Few people realize that our government provides home ownership opportunities to regular folks like you and me that are denied, or are just unobtainable, to most of the people in the rest of the world.

If you're looking into home ownership, you should definitely explore all the opportunities our government provides. Remember, however, that you must have good credit and a good credit history. Prior evictions or problems with landlords will blemish your record. You also must have the financial base to support the mortgage, utilities, assessments, and other costs of owning your own home.

Officers in the old Wild West movies about the U.S. Cavalry were always sending out scouts so that the troopers would be prepared for whatever lay ahead. You have to do your own scouting to make sure there are no unpleasant surprises around the next turn in the road. Check your credit rating. Mistakes often creep in, and you may have black marks against your name for which you are not responsible. Expunge them immediately.

Be prepared before you visit with a Realtor. Have all of your financial "ducks in a row" so that the Realtor's time will be invested in reality and not fantasy. There's no use looking at a $500,000 townhome if you qualify for only a $200,000 home. That's a waste of everyone's time and resources.

I have personal experience in this area. Before buying my first condo, I hadn't a clue as to what level I was qualified to purchase. The Realtor I used showed me a small multiunit property in which I could live and also derive a steady income from renting out the other units. The price was $125,000. That's a lot of money today, and it was a whole lot of money in 1982. Today, that property is probably worth about $800,000.

Unfortunately, I did not qualify to buy it. There were two problems:

1. I lacked a sufficient down payment
2. The price didn't adequately reflect the amount of renovation required to bring it into A-1 shape.

I couldn't qualify for financing, and on top of everything else, interest rates were at a whopping 14 percent in those days. Embarrassed, I had to ask the Realtor for a refund of my earnest money. After the poor guy had invested a lot of time and effort, he ended up with a big fat zero for all his effort. That was a real learning experience.

It's your responsibility to prepare yourself for the challenges of looking for, finding, negotiating for, and purchasing a new home. Do your homework and don't hesitate to call on your network of friends, family, and associates to help you meet those challenges.

An adage says that all the rules go out the window when you buy a home to live in. I don't buy that 100 percent, but it has great wisdom with moderation. Certainly you want to buy a home that will provide a good return on your investment, but dollars and cents shouldn't be your only reason for buying a home. You and your family are going to live in that dwelling for a considerable time. Buying solely on the basis of investment value will not be in your best interest.

Don't sacrifice quality of life, pride of ownership, comfort, and the pure enjoyment of a happy home just to make a few extra bucks. I've seen too many people buy an overpriced home in the hope it would appreciate dramatically over the years, only to see their investment flounder in a flat real estate economy. Be conservative and achieve a good balance between a return on your investment and the quality of your lifestyle.

BUYING FOR INVESTING

If you already have that happy home and are looking for capital appreciation or cash flow, then numerous opportunities exist to buy condos or townhomes as rental properties. Ownership is a great way to earn extra income, sometimes a substantial extra income. As always, you want to conduct a lot of in-depth research before you commit to a contract and financial obligations. For example, you'll want to make sure that you won't be saddled with a special assessment or any unanticipated and unknown financial burden.

Buying a unit as a "fixer-upper" isn't a bad way to enter the investment market.

THE OPTIONS
IN DETAIL

4

CONDOMINIUMS

"Almost any man worthy of his salt would fight to defend his home,
but no one ever heard of a man going to war for his boarding house."

Mark Twain

Owning your own home is something special. Home ownership has a powerful pull on the American mind, in part because in our nation it's such an achievable goal for so much of our population. Owning your own home is a bedrock element of the American dream, and the rest of the world marvels at how so many dreams come true here. For more and more people, condominiums, co-ops, and townhomes are the port of entry. Part II of this book examines these three opportunities, beginning with condos. Please remember that this is a general overview. Rules, regulations, laws, and definitions inevitably vary state by state, community by community, and even building by building. Use the information found here as a core of your research materials, but please do your own homework in your selected community.

The word *condominium* comes to us from the world-conquering Romans for whom it meant a common ownership of undivided fractional shares in a property. Condominiums, or condos, as a form of dwelling space have been around since the Middle Ages. They first appeared in the United States in the late 1800s as the nation's population was just beginning its long migration from farm and field to street and avenue. The lifestyle was popular because it combined the benefits of home ownership with the quality of life enjoyed by apartment dwellers. Condos didn't really take off, however, until the 1950s, when the Federal Housing Authority (FHA) sought to encourage home ownership in the cities by altering government regulations to permit FHA insurance on condo units. Suddenly, condos were not only desirable, but they were affordable and obtainable.

What exactly is a condominium? One of the most curious, yet most appropriate, definitions is "a box of air." Imagine a high-rise building segmented into condominium apartments. Box of air is a pretty accurate description, don't you think? To be a bit more specific, a condominium represents ownership in real property, in which the owner acquires title to that property and ownership of common areas with other owners in the same complex. A condo can be a lofty apartment in a high-rise building or it can be a townhome-style dwelling resting on solid ground.

Again, definitions vary, but here's a definition from Arizona's Department of Revenue that pretty well sizes up the matter. A condominium is "real estate, portions of which are designated for separate ownership and the remainder of which is designated for common ownership solely by the owners of the separate portions. Real estate is not a condominium unless the undivided interests in the common elements are vested in the unit owners." As you will see later in this chapter, common ownership and shared responsibilities are a major component of the condominium lifestyle.

A condominium is composed of three elements:

1. The living space
2. Joint ownership of common areas, such as exterior walls, mechanical elements supporting the entire complex, walkways, and common green areas
3. Easements to adjust the precise location of an owner's living space should the building settle through natural means

We think of condos as individual or family living spaces, and that's generally true, but you'll find condo subdivisions containing commercial and even industrial property. The latter two don't concern us here, but I thought I'd give you a warning, although a business operating in your development isn't automatically in violation of the association's regulations.

WHO OWNS WHAT

The most significant difference between condominium and town-home ownership on one hand and ownership of a single-family residential dwelling on the other involves ownership of the land. When you buy a single-family home, you also buy the land on which it rests. Condo owners purchase joint ownership of all the land in the development, an undivided interest in each unit. In addition, a condominium must be legally identified by the word *condominium* in the name of the development, or the word must appear in the declaration that legally creates the project. It's not a condo unless you call it a condo.

This is an important point and one not to be ignored. Condominiums are creations of law and not merely a way to describe the physical attributes of a particular structure or set of structures. As a rule of thumb, a buyer purchases the residential structure and a proportional share of common walls. Check this matter out carefully, because in some instances the owner purchases only the air space within the residential structure. A box of air then is often more than just a fanciful definition.

When you purchase your individual unit, you also purchase a proportionate share of the common areas with the other owners. It's included as part of a package of ownership rights; you own and have access to, the common areas. Naturally, however, you give up certain rights of ownership; for example, you don't have the right to sell, rent, trade, or subdivide the common areas. You can't sell a wall or the heating and cooling unit, rent a door or window, or trade a sidewalk or a tree. I think you'll agree that's not much of a sacrifice.

LAND VALUES

Condominiums may differ from other forms of ownership in the market by definition, but they reflect, and are affected by, the marketplace. The same market forces that increase, decrease, or maintain the value of a single-family dwelling are working just as efficiently and effectively on condos, co-ops, and townhomes. The laws of supply and demand are always at work.

Density (the number of people within the development) is a major factor in assessing value. The density of the authorized use under the appropriate condominium zoning regulations tends to support a land value per comparative unit higher than the per unit value of single-family residential land. Developers in most states invest similarly in condos and single-family dwellings in such areas as site preparation, roads within the development, and sidewalks. Market forces require that developers of condominiums build competitive structures if they wish to sell property. This is, of course, a generalization. Again, markets vary, so be sure to carefully investigate every aspect of any development you are considering.

No rule of thumb exists as a guide to how many units can be placed within a given space—say an acre. Some developments may have as few as 2 or 3 units per acre, whereas others may have as many as 15. Most seem to fall into the category of 7 to 10 units per acre. Low or high density is neither good nor bad per se; it depends on the individual development. Density does have an affect on cost but not in direct proportion to the number of units per acre. It stands to reason that constructing 10 units will run up costs more than will 7 units. On the other hand, the more units per acre, the lower the cost per unit. For example, if site preparation is $30,000 per acre and the developer builds 6 units, the preparation cost per unit is $5,000 ($30,000 divided by 6 = $5,000). If a developer is planning to build 4 units per acre and the site preparation costs are a lower $24,000, the cost per unit is a larger $6,000 ($24,000 divided by 4 = $6,000). These are hypothetical figures just to give you an idea of how things work.

BE PREPARED BEFORE YOU BUY

Purchasing a condo is significantly different from buying a single-family dwelling. You're actually purchasing two very different properties. In a condo purchase, you're buying the space in which you will live, but you're also buying property held in common with other owners. An old series of commercials for chewing gum promised, "Double your pleasure, double your fun," a promise that can also apply to the purchase of a condominium. But if you don't do adequate research well in advance, you could just as easily double your headaches. Let's look at the ways we can make your purchase a doubly pleasurable one.

Always look beneath the surface. That advice applies to contracts and agreements as well as to ceilings, walls, and floors. Too many people base their decisions on the floor plan, proximity to certain amenities, or just the "feel" of the place. Those are important considerations, but they shouldn't be the bedrock of your decision. A great floor plan is worthless if the floor isn't sound and will require substantial renovation. The physical properties of a structure are more than the way they appear. Remember my earlier warning that beauty is skin deep, but ugly goes all the way to the bone. It's important that you get a good look at the "bones" of any property you're considering. Areas of concern include the quality of the following:

- Roof and ceiling
- Walls
- Floors and flooring
- Siding
- Subsoil conditions
- Potential for flooding
- Air-conditioning systems
- Heating systems
- Plumbing
- Electrical systems and wiring
- Windows and doors
- Elevators
- Common walkways, stairs, halls, etc.
- Appliances

Granted that while an in-depth knowledge of these areas is outside the range of most buyers' experience, there's still a lot you can do. You have two key defensive weapons at your disposal. One, sellers are required by law to make specific declarations about the quality of the properties they represent. You'll get a legal document detailing the condition of the property, but that's not enough. Some problems that may not manifest themselves until later aren't legally problems at the moment of sale, so you still need an expert's advice. That's the second defensive weapon: hiring an inspector. You don't want to hire someone for every property; that's just a waste of money. But when you narrow your choice to "the" house, it's a waste of money *not* to hire an inspector. This professional can save you thousands of dollars or more by spotting potential problems you can have the owner fix before you move in. An inspector can also provide peace of mind with a clean bill of health on your desired property. You can move in confident that no structural nightmares are waiting to awaken you in the middle of the night. Believe me, the expense of an inspector is minimal compared with what he or she can save you over the long run.

LOOKING AT NEW CONSTRUCTION

You have two choices of condo properties: new and existing. Many concerns overlap, but each also has its own set of concerns. Whenever you're looking at a property under construction, remember there can be a world of difference between the fanciful descriptions of a salesperson and the hard realities of a prospectus. I'm not implying that all salespeople are con artists, but their job is to paint a sales picture in the rosiest possible terms. Sometimes the paint gets slapped on with a rather broad brush. The bottom line is to believe the written word over the spoken. Even then, double-check the fine print.

The warning applies to newspaper and magazine advertising, corporate brochures, video programs, and presentations on CDs and computers. These are fine as far as they go, which sometimes isn't very far, but you don't want to base your decisions on anything other than legal documents.

Your prospectus will include a section titled "Description of Property," which of course describes the property and outlines the developer's responsibilities to the buyers. A number of fairly consistent areas exist where the developer's prospectus may vary from the brochures, ads, and sales pitches. A few items you should always check out are described in the following paragraphs.

The quality of components is always a big question and runs the gamut from stoves and refrigerators through windows and doors to carpet and paint. You can do a lot of qualifying on your own and in a surprisingly short amount of time. Here's how. The prospectus notes the manufacturer and model number of specific elements of the condominium under construction: type of doors and windows, stove, water heater, bathroom fixtures, and so on. You can easily look up a local supplier in the phone book, call the company, and ask about the quality of those specific products. You should be able to get a good idea whether the components are top-of-the-line, of average quality, or below par. That's a lot of valuable information. If a lot of the items are in the below-par list, that lack of quality might be reflected in every aspect of the structure. Keep in mind that it's not necessarily bad if a lot of elements wind up in the average column. Adequate doesn't mean poor or defective. Just make sure the price of your condo is in the adequate column too. Don't pay for top-of-the-line components unless you're getting them.

Frames on most low-rise developments are usually wood with concrete slabs. Some frames are wooden 2 × 4s, others are 2 × 6s, and some are steel. All can represent solid quality construction, but it's a good idea to know what you're buying just the same.

Siding can vary as can its quality. Pine wood is the least expensive siding, cedar the most costly. Vinyl is cheaper than wood and maintenance is much easier. Plywood is generally not as strong as wood, but even here exceptions exist. Brick is also popular. What represents quality? Also important is what represents your idea of an attractive home. Before sacrificing the brick you want, think about how you'll feel about that pine next year, three years down the road, or even a decade later. You're going to live in that condo, so make sure it's what you consider livable.

You'll want to investigate the common areas, such as the roadways, sidewalks, retaining walls, and drainage systems. What is the quality of construction? Who retains ownership? Will the condo owners keep the common areas or will they be ceded to the community? Again, always read the prospectus carefully and ask questions if you don't find the answers you want. You will live with the results of your actions (or lack of actions) for some time.

Landscaping is another area of concern. Your documentation will list specifics such as type and number of trees, bushes, or shrubs to be planted; whether the soil will be sod or seeded topsoil; whether you'll be provided with an underground watering system; and so on. Upgrades might even be possible at an additional cost. All of this information and more should be disclosed to you. Make sure what you see on paper reflects what you'll actually see outside your windows.

Recreational facilities should be described in detail down to floor plans of any "rec" buildings; the number and type of equipment to be installed; the type of lighting, if any; a description of construction materials (black top or clay tennis courts, for example); and other details. Never assume that you're getting the full story. Ask questions, lots of questions, and make sure you're satisfied with the answers before making a commitment.

The prospectus should list the appliances included in the property, including the brand name and model number. Again, you can check out the quality with a few phone calls. Keep in mind that the developer often retains the right to substitute brands and model numbers provided that the substitution is of equal quality to that listed in the document. You might even have the option to upgrade or add appliances if you sign an agreement in the earlier stages. Of course, you can expect to pay extra for the extra conveniences.

Look carefully at the plans for the condo. Some plans have been known to omit closets and pantries to make the rooms look bigger on paper. Sure, you buy the same amount of square feet, but when the closets are added, your actual living space decreases. Watch for phrases such as "the interior design shall be substantially similar" to the drawings, which means the developer has pretty much of a free reign to make a lot of changes, some of which you might consider radical. It's your responsibility, so make sure the condo you move into is the one for which you signed the contract.

Check the condominium charges. After all, because the structure hasn't been completed, you have no way to know the precise expenses. Estimates have to be used, but, unfortunately, some developers are notorious for underestimating such costs, which may include garbage disposal, common area insurance, electricity expenses for common areas, water, upkeep of the exterior areas and landscaping, legal and accounting fees, and financial reserves for future maintenance and repair. Before you commit anything to paper, ask around the neighborhood at similar developments so you can "compare apples to apples."

Don't forget parking. If it's not included in the prospectus, it's probably not included in the deal. You might end up having to rent parking from the developer. Whenever you look at plans and architectural renderings, it's a good idea to ask yourself, "What am I *not* seeing here?" If something's not there, chances are you'll end up paying extra to put it in the picture.

LOOKING AT EXISTING PROPERTY

There's an upside and a downside to existing property. Each may or may not be significant when looking at any given building, but you should always consider the relevant factors. On the downside, an existing building has been lived in and will probably show varying degrees of wear and tear. Only you can determine which degree is acceptable for your budget and lifestyle. On the upside, you're buying a known quantity and can examine the real thing in its entirety. You can "kick the tires," so to speak. You can ask current and previous owners what they liked and didn't like. Handled correctly and with care, looking at an existing property can mean that you won't face any unexpected and unpleasant surprises after you move in, which doesn't mean you won't have any problems. Every homeowner has challenges, even those in brand-new dwellings.

Developers of existing properties are required by law to make certain disclosures about the quality of those properties. Always read this information carefully and follow up with pointed questions. Get all the information you need. That's your responsibility, not the developer's or his or her salespeople. Remember that the disclosure applies to items not visible to an inspecting engineer or that has come about as a result of complaints or comments from the owners. Disclosure of a defect doesn't necessarily mean that the developer is obligated to correct that defect. Most existing properties will have some defects; that's natural. The question is, Will the developer make the repairs? Will you make the repairs, or can you live with the situation? Here are a few areas for you to investigate.

TRIPS, TRAPS, AND TREASURE

A buyer should examine a condo, co-op, or townhome like a detective examining a crime scene. You don't want to miss a single clue. There may be defects that could trip you up later on during your occupancy, traps that could tie you into a contract not in your favor, or the occasional treasure that means you've found what you're looking for. Basically, you have to look around, get documentation, and ask questions.

You'll find more paperwork around than you probably realize. Be sure to track it down and examine it with a fine-tooth comb. First, ask the seller and/or broker for a list of defects and tenant complaints. Acquire, or acquire access to, minutes from the board of directors' meetings where such matters have been discussed. The latest financial report may contain valuable information about repairs to defects or financial allocations for maintenance and repair of such defects. You can also inquire with the municipal building departments for notices of building code violations.

Defects or needed repairs in and of themselves needn't represent red flags. Any existing property will probably have some defects, maintenance problems, and items needing repair. That's to be expected. As a potential buyer, however, you should make yourself aware of these items, especially any expensive repairs that might require additional assessments. The most expensive areas to maintain and repair for most buildings are these:

- Defects in the façade, such as weakening mortar
- Roof
- Elevator(s)
- Plumbing
- Electrical systems
- Boiler replacements
- Significant cosmetic upgrades

You can also conduct a good bit of on-site testing yourself. Here's a list of things to do that apply to new and existing construction as well as to condos, co-ops, and townhomes.

- Test all the appliances.
- Use the plumbing fixtures to make sure they work and there is enough water pressure and sufficient drainage.
- Check the central air-conditioning unit or window units.
- Check the heating system to make sure the temperature matches the thermostat setting. Use a thermometer to measure the heat throughout each room to be sure the system is heating properly throughout and not just near the ducts.
- Feel under the air ducts to make sure the air flow is really flowing.
- Look at the electrical wiring for loose wires, frayed cords, aging cords or connections, and the like.

- Look up and look down to detect any signs of water leakage in the ceiling or floors. Don't forget to look carefully in the basement.
- Check for cracks in the concrete. Some thin cracks occur naturally when concrete dries and shrinks, but ask if you have any doubts.
- Work all the doors and cabinets to see that they open and close easily.
- Climb up to the attic to examine the insulation and any signs of roof leakage and to determine that the air vents work properly.
- If there's a fireplace, check to make sure it draws properly by burning a sheet of newspaper in it.
- Read your prospectus and property description to make sure that you see exactly what you have read.
- Create a punch list, a written list of defects found during your walk-through. The seller is obligated to correct these defects before the closing. If the work has to be completed after closing, the list and any related papers should become part of the closing documents. If there is a dispute between buyer and seller over a particular item, you have the right to request a written statement from the seller's architect or engineer that the defect is in fact not a defect or that it is not a significant matter.
- Take a look at your neighbors. Are they individuals, young families, mature families, or seniors? Is this the environment you want?

CONDOMINIUM ASSOCIATIONS

As previously noted, purchasing a condo means buying into shared responsibilities, and that's where the condominium association comes into play. The association is created by a document called the Declaration of Condominium Property Regime filed with the appropriate municipal authority. This document defines the ownership into two categories: the living space owned by individual purchasers and the common areas owned by all. The individual living spaces are owned separately and can be sold separately.

Note that the association does not own the common areas. They are owned jointly by the people who have purchased their property and have joined the association.

It's important that you research the financial stability of any association you may have to join. The management of this organization has a tremendous amount of power over the quality of your life while you are a member. Members of management are the ones who will decide when the roof needs repair, when the heating and air-conditioning system needs replacement, when the tennis courts need a new surface, when new lighting will be installed in the hallways, and so on. Make sure there are enough financial reserves to cover these and the other expenses that will inevitably arise.

Read the documents and ask other owners. How well and how quickly does the association respond to their needs? Does the association adhere to high standards for maintenance and repair? Are the contractors and subcontractors reliable? What type of, and how much, insurance does the association carry? Have any lawsuits been filed against it? How does the organization respond to special requests or needs? Are the owners happy, relatively happy, or dissatisfied with the association? How much maintenance is included in your monthly fee? What is the structure of the association?

You have probably heard of homeowners associations, sometimes called community associations. These relate to homeowners and differ significantly from condominium associations. Homeowner associations are created when a developer sets up a group of restrictions relative to the land and housing within the development. These are called covenants, conditions, and restrictions, (CC&Rs), and they set limits on what homeowners are allowed to do with or on their property. For example, exterior paint colors may be limited to a narrow range, storage sheds may be prohibited, certain types of doors may be required, and landscaping may be strictly controlled. Such requirements can be quite extensive. I know of a home in which the owner painted his exterior according to CC&R requirements, even using the paint and painting contractor recommended by his association. Sunlight faded the paint, effectively changing the color, and the owner was slapped with a fine for having a prohibited color! I've even read of CC&R being enforced to keep people from flying a large American flag, or preventing grandparents from taking in grandkids orphaned by tragedy.

A homeowners association is generally a nonprofit corporation. Although the members enjoy many of the rights of shareholders in a traditional corporation, technically they are not shareholders. Also, here the association does own the common areas, although members have full access to them.

Home ownership is central to the achievement of the American dream and condominium ownership is often the best first step. As Mark Twain said, it is something worth fighting for. When you are considering the purchase of a condominium, co-op, or townhome, it is essential that you take your time, do your homework, and ask the tough questions before you sign the contract. That's the best way to make sure you're fighting for something that's really worth the effort.

5

CO-OPS

Buying into a Corporation

*"Coming together is a beginning; keeping together
is progress; working together is success."*

Henry Ford

A cooperative, or co-op, is a corporation; you own shares in the corporation when you become an owner, but the corporation owns the property. As one of many owners, you are allowed a specific living space plus other units of space within, or a part of, the complex. It is the corporation that finances the project, acquires the mortgage, and owns the building and any associated amenities. This is a significant difference, so let me repeat. As a member of a co-op, you are the owner of shares in a corporation, which is considerably different from owning a dwelling (a box of air) and the land on which it rests.

Co-ops and condos remain very popular among America's homebuyers. According to the National Association of Realtors, sales for cooperatives and condominiums remained at "exceptionally high" levels at midyear 2002, with "unprecedented activity, far above any previous records."[1] First-quarter sales for condos and co-ops during the first quarter of 2002 hit a record of 837,000 units with 831,000 units sold during the second quarter.

Although association living is attractive to first-time homeowners, the purchase of a co-op or condominium is also attractive to investment buyers. According to a NAR economist, price appreciation was twice the rate of single-family homes.[2] Condos and co-ops are particularly popular in the South and the West. Here's a look at sales for 2002 by region, again from NAR statistics.

- 376,000 units sold in the South
- 225,000 units sold in the West
- 137,000 units sold in the Northeast
- 94,000 units sold in the Midwest

MEMBERSHIP MEANS ACTIVE PARTICIPATION

Buying into the corporation means participating in the corporation. Again, co-op living has a lot to do with shared responsibility. You have to accept some of that responsibility to make sure things run smoothly. Among your corporate duties are:

- The initial purchase of shares that grants you membership
- Payment of your monthly assessment or fees
- Attending the regular business meetings of the corporation with the other owners
- Taking an active role in managing the affairs of the co-op

Any number of ways are available for you to become involved in your co-op, and you don't have to be a politician to participate. A member has the right to run for membership on the board of directors, volunteer as a member of a committee or to head a committee, or form a committee that is needed. Some people who have green thumbs or who are good with tools volunteer to perform landscaping or maintenance and repair work. A co-op may be a corporation, but it is made up of people, and people enjoy getting to know each other. You might find your niche in the social committee or in similar duties.

You will have many opportunities to get involved, and I encourage you to. You'll be accepting your share of responsibilities, you'll have a say-so in how your co-op is run, and you'll get to meet a lot of great people. This amount of work is obviously time consuming. To me, it's all worth the time and effort, but you have to make a serious commitment.

That's certainly something to consider before making the big purchasing commitment and signing that contract.

You'll notice a number of differences between co-op housing and rentals or ownership. Here are a few examples. Co-op monthly fees are set by the corporation; that is, the members (owners) determine their own payments. Rental payments are set by the landlord and paid by the renters. Homeowners must cover the cost of their mortgage, utilities, and any other fees themselves. Owners and landlords earn the profits from their investments. A co-op has profits in the form of increased value of its shares. No profits are earned or shared by the members. A down payment is required to purchase a home, and renters also make a down payment, often in the form of a damage deposit or the last month's rent. Co-op members are not required to make a down payment, but they do have to purchase their shares in the corporation. Homeowners are responsible for their own maintenance, whereas renters depend on the landlord to handle maintenance responsibilities. Co-op maintenance and repair are the responsibility of the corporation, but members are often actively involved.

When leaving, both renters and co-op members must give notice according to their lease agreement; a homeowner has to sell his or her property.

FEES

Of course, fees vary from co-op to co-op, even within the same market. A more upscale or luxury complex will have more and higher costs than a more modest development. Always shop around within your price range. Dreaming is okay, but a practical assessment of your ability to maintain your lifestyle is essential. Remember, you have time to acquire more wealth. Moving up is also a major component of the American dream.

Co-op maintenance fees are significantly higher than are fees for condominiums. A rule of thumb is 50 percent higher, with the reason obvious and justified. Condo fees have to cover only maintenance and repair of the common areas. Co-op fees cover a good bit more, including mortgage payments, real estate taxes, utility bills, water bills, heating and cooling charges, upkeep of common areas, and other costs of the labor involved. You pay more because you get more.

Another significant difference between co-ops and condos is that condominium associations have their own particular benefits and challenges. For example, membership is democracy in action. Everyone has a say. Everyone has a vote. But what happens when a tornado creates substantial damage to the roof. The condo board can call the local bank or S&L to get a loan for repairing the damage. The assessment acts as receivables to collateralize the loan. Sometimes a meeting of the members must be called and a vote taken, and this is where democracy gets tricky. The vote to obtain a loan must be unanimous. Suppose a few hardheads living on the lower floors aren't affected by the roof damage. If they vote against getting a loan, then there is no loan. This is a good example of why our Founding Fathers founded a representative republic and not a pure democracy. If the motion to get the loan fails because of dissenters, the condo may have to use the corporation's cash flow to pay for the repairs, which can be a costly matter in the long run.

The situation is vastly different and much more efficient in a co-op. If there's a need for a major capital improvement, such as putting on a new roof, then the board can vote to take out a second mortgage to cover the expense. It's much more difficult for hardheads to control a co-op; individual owners have far less power to cause trouble.

Speaking of troublemakers, it's far easier to handle them within a co-op than it is in a condo association. If the owner of a condo unit becomes delinquent in paying his or her assessment, removing that individual or family could take up to two years. First, a lien must be placed against the unit. Then official foreclosure proceedings must be initiated. Meanwhile, the owner can continue to live within the unit, sometimes snubbing his or her nose at the other owners, honorable people who are making the effort to make their payments.

Things can move a lot faster in a co-op. If someone becomes delinquent, the owner can be served with a notice to dispossess, and the troublesome person(s) can be evicted almost immediately.

Insurance isn't actually a fee, but it's a financial matter all co-op owners should consider. Your co-op will, of course, carry insurance. The problem is that the organization may not carry enough to repair your unit fully in the event of a serious problem. Suppose a tornado really does hit, or the co-op suffers a fire, a flood, or some other catastrophe, and you discover that you have to make up the difference to bring your unit back up to 100 percent. The costs could be extensive.

A wise and economical way to handle a catastrophe is to have supplemental insurance. Add it to your policy that covers the contents of your unit. The cost is minimal compared with what you could spend after a tornado decides to take a close look at the inside of your home.

DISCRIMINATION IS A THING OF THE PAST, RIGHT?

Officially, yes. No one can be denied the right to purchase shares in a co-op because of his or her race, nationality, creed, or color. New categories, such as sexual orientation, are being added constantly. In reality, discrimination goes on all the time. For example, if members object to someone because of his national origin, they don't state that reason publicly. Other reasons are used, reasons that are not prohibited, and the individual is denied membership. Whatever you choose to call it, the result is the same—discrimination.

I tend to agree with Tryon Edwards, who said, "He that is possessed with a prejudice is possessed with a devil." Nonetheless, it is a fact of life throughout the world, and the world of real estate is not exempt.

6

TOWNHOMES
The Middle Ground

"We are surrounded by insurmountable opportunities."

Walt Kelly

Walt Kelly was a master cartoonist-philosopher, the creator of Pogo Possum and other critters in the Okefenokee swamp. As the above quote proves, his characters had a way of completely twisting the English language and yet still come up with simple, powerful truths. When it comes to purchasing a home in America, we are truly surrounded by opportunity. That applies whether you're a young couple buying a starter home, an older couple downsizing after the kids have moved on, or someone looking for investment property. It's all here and it's all available.

Lots of people are looking at the opportunity provided by ownership of a townhome. There are lots of reasons too. One is the rising cost of single-family dwellings. Surveys show that rising costs are a major factor motivating people to purchase older homes instead of new construction, buying smaller homes instead of larger ones, remodeling an existing home, or continuing to rent.[1] The affordability of many townhomes provides an answer to rising costs without requiring the sacrifice of a satisfactory quality of life.

Other factors besides costs favor the purchase of a townhome. For example, many people, especially those with families, are finding the suburbs more stressful than they had originally believed. As the suburbs expand further from the city and sources of employment, workers are forced into longer and longer commutes and thus cuts dramatically into quality time with the family. Many people are understandably unwilling to make that sacrifice. Urban living in a townhome (or condo or co-op) closer to one's job permits less driving time and creates more time for the family. The city's proximity to more cultural, entertainment, and recreational outlets is another plus.

Townhomes are popular with young families just starting out and with empty nesters who no longer need a larger home and are attracted to urban communities with lots of amenities and where someone else takes care of maintenance and upkeep. According to the U.S. Bureau of the Census, about 70 percent of the population could be living in homes without children by 2010.[2]

Home ownership is deeply embedded in the American dream, and these days we see a lot of dreaming going on. Nearly 70 percent of U.S. households are owned by the people living in them. According to the 11th National Housing Survey by Fannie Mae, the following groups plan to purchase a home within the next three years:[3]

- 42 percent of African Americans
- 37 percent of Hispanics
- 31 percent of baby boomers

Many of those folks will be conducting walk-throughs of townhomes.

LIVING IN AN ANCIENT TRADITION

A townhome is defined as a dwelling unit, usually consisting of two or more floors, attached to similar dwellings by common walls called "party walls." The height rarely exceeds three to five stories for a good reason. In the days before elevators, that was considered the maximum number of stairs an individual could comfortably walk on a daily basis. Townhomes, primarily a facet of urban living, were considered for many years a major building block of the city and may just be making a major comeback.

If you decide to enter association living through the door of a townhome, you will be entering a bit of history. Townhomes date back as far as the ancient Roman Empire. In fact, many of Pompeii's dwellings, buried for centuries under the volcanic ash of Mt. Vesuvius, were townhomes and would easily be recognized as such today. The Roman town house consisted of a number of elements that varied according to the wishes of the owner and the recommendations of the architect, but generally included:

- A wall facing the street
- An entrance facing the street
- A hallway or transition space from the street to the main house
- An atrium or central open space with high walls
- A master bedroom
- A room for family records (an office)
- A garden in the rear (today's backyard)

The intent of this design was to lead the owner from an urban environment—the street—to a form of the country life—the garden. If a Roman family from Pompeii were to come for a visit to your townhome, it might not recognize your computer, DVD player, or refrigerator, but it would certainly feel comfortable and at home in the overall environment.

Townhomes remained popular through the Middle Ages but came back into their own in London during the mid-1800s. The style was quickly adopted by England's American cousins and would have been quite familiar to any ancient Roman architect. These homes bridged the classic designs from the past to the requirements and economy of a modern, industrialized, urban lifestyle. Typically, the homes were long and narrow, leading from the street-facing front door through the home to a garden or backyard and a service alley. They were often called "terrace houses" and were sometimes three or four stories high. One floor was for dining, one for sleeping, a third for guests and entertaining, a fourth for the kitchen, and sometimes a fifth level to house the servants.

Although many architectural styles have been used and continue to be used, modified, and created, the basic townhome design has remained constant for a couple of thousand years.

Townhome living in the United States renewed its popularity in the 1970s. The vast movement to the suburbs had kicked suburban home prices into high gear. As inflation and other factors priced many people out of the market, particularly young families and couples just starting out, the smaller, less expensive, and maintenance-free attraction of townhome living started pulling people back into the city. Zoning allowed multi-unit dwellings, land was scarce, and builders could buy land reasonably when building multiple dwellings.

As more people returned to the urban environment, the nature of the townhouse changed to accommodate new requirements of new residents. Today, the newly constructed homes are often larger than their predecessors. They may have two-car garages, more bedrooms or more bedroom space, more baths or at least an additional half-bath, and may be designed to resemble single-family detached dwellings. Older homes may have their challenges. What does a 20th century owner do with a small, 19th-century butler's chamber? The owner might convert that space into an additional closet or just open it up to make a larger room. Creative challenges can be met with . . . creativity.

YOU BUY THE HOUSE, YOU BUY THE LAND

The chief difference between buying a townhome and a condominium is that you also buy the land beneath the townhome just as you would with a single-family dwelling. Although there are similarities, remember that a condo must be legally declared a "condominium." Also, the land in a condominium development is owned in common with each owner having an undivided interest in each parcel of land.

Townhouses are usually constructed to resemble typical residential condominium developments, but there are significant differences. A townhome complex is more accurately described as a planned unit development (PUD), a development clearly defined by the subdivision's conditions, covenants, and restrictions, (those previously mentioned CC&Rs). In addition to townhomes, a PUD may include commercial and industrial properties as well as detached single-family dwellings.

When you purchase a townhome, you usually purchase the land beneath it. You might also purchase a small parcel of land to the front, rear, and sides—a small yard. Other land within the development, such as sidewalks, recreational outlets, and other common areas, are owned in common by an owners association that is managed by the owners. This is a general rule of thumb, so you may see slight variations from community to community. Always get the full story in writing on any property you're considering buying.

The terms *condominium* and *condo* are often used interchangeably with *townhome* or *townhouse*. Even though this may be convenient, it is also highly inaccurate. The terms describe entirely different entities. In most cases, a townhome owner owns the living space within the structure and a proportionate share of the party (common) walls; a parcel number is assigned to each individual townhome. A condo is also assigned a parcel number, but the owner does not receive separate title to his or her (jointly owned) land.

As noted earlier, townhome living has seen a strong resurgence of interest in the United States, especially since the 1970s. The trend seems to be continuing, and allowing for the inevitable ups and downs of the market, it should remain strong for some time to come. Across the board, Americans of all ages, incomes, and backgrounds are seeing the "insurmountable opportunity" facing them in the form of townhome living.

MAKING THE BUY

7

FINANCING

"The closing is only as good as the money the borrower brings to the table."

Mark B. Weiss

An often repeated adage states, "Money talks." It's true, but in America money shouts, especially for people buying condos, co-ops, and townhomes. When someone asks, "What's all the shouting about?" they're referring to money—specifically financing. Financing is the mechanism that allows people to own their own home. It provides the fuel for the real estate engine, and for more than a decade that engine has powered an enormous segment of the U.S. economy.

THE MAGIC OF OPM

Before I ever contemplated building my own company, I had heard that the key to success in any business is OPM—other people's money. Risk someone else's money on your venture rather than your own. Of course, part of the arrangement is to pay the lender interest on that money. The use of OPM should always be a win-win situation for both parties. I remember that some of the people who used the phrase spoke it as if it were some magic incantation. Well, it may not be magic, but in real estate OPM can have near magical effects.

When you purchase your home, you'll use other people's money in the form of a mortgage. A mortgage is a written instrument (contract) that allows you to use your newly acquired real estate as collateral against the loan you use to purchase that real estate. As the borrower, someone who pledges that property to secure the loan, you are the *mortgagor*. The financial institution, such as a bank, a savings and loan, or a mortgage loan company, providing the money for your purchase is the *mortgagee*. Sometimes home financing is arranged through a third party called a *mortgage broker*.

Some lending institutions do double duty and act as a broker. It's important to know whether a broker is involved in your transaction, because brokers charge a fee that may be in addition to fees charged by the lender. If a broker is involved, find out how this individual or company will be compensated. Frequently, brokers' fees are in the form of *points*, a percentage of the loan principal, whereby one point usually equals 1 percent of the amount of the principal. Obviously, it's important to know the extent of your financial obligation, but it is equally prudent to know how those funds are distributed in the form of principal, interest, charges, fees, and possible penalties.

Few of us have the financial strength to purchase a home on our own. Fortunately, we have access to organizations that not only have money but are more than willing to lend it to worthy individuals and families. That's what a lot of the shouting is all about. Hooray!

SHOP AROUND

Some time ago I encountered a fellow earning a substantial income. He was so proud of his earnings that he sought means of conspicuous consumption just to impress people. As one of his friends said, "He pays sticker price and is *proud* of it." Few of us earn that kind of income or are so foolish with the ways we spend it. We shop around. Whether we're looking for a new car, a kitchen stove, a new suit, or a home, we seek out and try to arrange the best deal.

It's only prudent to apply the same principle to acquiring a mortgage for two sound reasons. One is that although what you'll find at one lending institution is pretty much the same as you'll find at another, differences do exist. A small percentage saved here or there can make an enormous difference in real dollars over time. Also, by shopping around you'll meet a lot of different real estate professionals; and as in any business, some folks are better at their job than others. Why not seek out the best? The second reason for trying to arrange the best deal is that predatory lenders are out there and will take advantage of inexperienced borrowers. Shopping around gives you a sound base from which to make comparisons.

Traditionally, lending institutions would not loan the full purchase price of a property; the breakdown is 80/20. The loan covers 80 percent of the amount with the borrower responsible for the remaining 20 percent as a down payment. That's changing, however, and some lenders today are requiring as little as 5 percent down on a conventional loan.

Too many people assume they can't wheel and deal with a real estate professional, but that's not always the case. Market conditions may make it so, but market conditions may also make people in the industry more than willing to work with buyers. It never hurts to try a bit of negotiation. If your efforts don't work out, you're no worse off, so why not give it a try? Ask if the lender or broker will lower the rate a point or two, or if some of the fees can be reduced or even eliminated. Make sure everything is in writing and that you understand that writing. You don't want to negotiate a reduced fee here only to have another fee raised over there.

A fundamental rule of life is that things change. For example, if loan rates rise after you've made an agreement but before your paperwork is completed, you could end up paying the higher rate. For that reason, many people get a *lock-in* from their lender or broker. As the name implies, a lock-in locks your interest rate in place regardless of changes in the market. This is somewhat of a gamble because interest rates could drop, and you'd remain locked in to the higher rate. Examine the trends in your market carefully to make sure any lock-in will probably remain in your favor. A fee is often charged for a lock-in, but it may be refunded when you close.

During the 1990s, 100 percent mortgages became more common. A 100 percent mortgage allows you to buy your property without a down payment. Such a mortgage does have limitations, and borrowers must have good credit. These are very popular with first-time buyers, who may not have been employed long enough to build up enough cash reserves for a down payment.

PMI: PRIVATE MORTGAGE INSURANCE

If you qualify for a loan with a payment less than 20 percent, you'll be required to purchase private mortgage insurance (PMI). This is an additional cost added to your monthly mortgage payment, ¹⁄₁₂ (one month) of your real estate taxes, and your monthly association assessment (see Figure 7.1). Private mortgage insurance provides your lending institution security for its funds when a borrower has little or no equity in the purchased property.

As with most things, there's an upside and a downside. The down is the additional cost of the insurance, which is not too bad when you consider the up, which is that PMI allows many people who don't have a down payment a way to purchase a home, and it can cut the waiting time by years. As you build equity over time, you will reach a point at which you no longer need the insurance; many people, in fact, reach this point after only a year. You should certainly start looking at the possibility of refinancing and dropping your PMI during that time frame. The first person you should consult is the lender or mortgage broker who arranged your original financing.

Even though PMI is a great advantage in helping you get into a new home, it's an advantage you should work to get out of as soon as possible. Let's say you have put $10,000 down on a $100,000 home. Because you haven't reached the 20 percent threshold, you have to purchase private mortgage insurance, which runs $40 a month. That's a modest sum and a small price to pay considering you got into your new condo, co-op, or townhome without having to fork over the full 20 percent down payment. But $40 a month is $480 a year, and that amount can become substantial over time. Check with your lender to determine your PMI payment, and start planning for the moment when you can forgo paying for this advantage.

The Homeowners Protection Act, which went into effect in 1999, set specific guidelines regarding borrower cancellation or automatic termination of PMI. Certain consumer protection was provided governing the purchase, initial construction, or refinancing of a single-family home. The act does not apply to government FHA or VA loans insured by the government or to private mortgage insurance covered by a lender.

FIGURE 7.1 *Cost of Ownership*

HOMETRUST

5% down $12,500	5-year ARM	Sales Price $250,000

Mortgage $237,500
4.375% (rates subject to change daily)

Principal & Interest	1,185.81
Taxes Est.	325.00
PMI	152.00
	$1,662.81

EASY APPLICATION PROCESS!

Estimated Funds for Closing

Down Payment		12,500
Lender Closing Costs		
Appraisal & Credit	300	
Underwriting	350	
Funding Fee	150	
Tax Service Fee	80	
Flood Certification	35	915
Title Ins. & Closing Fee Est.		500
City Stamps		1,875
Escrows and Est. Interim Interest		433
		$16,873

10-minute phone interview and documents e-mailed or faxed directly to you.

Donna Walstrom 847-902-4009

DWALSTROM@HOMETRUSTMORTGAGE.COM
FAX 847-557-9175

*YOUR NUMBER ONE LOAN OFFICER THAT YOU CAN TRUST
OVER 15 YEARS EXPERIENCE!*

Provided that your mortgage payments are current:

- Your PMI will be automatically cancelled when you reach 22 percent equity in your home based on the home's original value.
- You can request cancellation of your PMI when you reach 20 percent equity based on your home's original value.

There are, however, three basic exceptions to these provisions:

1. If within the prior year you haven't maintained current status on your loan payments
2. If yours is a high-risk loan
3. If there are additional liens against your property

PMI is a boon. It allows many people, especially young families, to own their own home earlier than possible before PMI. It's a good thing, but a good thing you should drop as soon as it is financially feasible. There's no reason to pay for something you no longer need when you could put that money in checking and savings accounts, investments, college or vacation funds, or toward a bigger and better condo, co-op, or townhome.

THE AMORTIZATION TABLE

The amortization table isn't some mythical gathering place for the knights of King Arthur. Amortization is a gradual paying off of a loan in increments, and the amortization table is a chart showing those payments, interest and principal requirements, and unpaid loan balances for the loan on a yearly basis. Amortization is a way you can spread your loan payments over a number of years, usually 30 years or even 15 years for those in a hurry to get out from under a mortgage.

Thirty years seems like a long time today, but that's not the case historically. People often purchased a home, usually their second, and lived in it the rest of their life. Many generations often lived in the same dwelling. I have an associate whose family has inhabited the same farm since the 1850s. Things move at a faster pace today, especially for families moving up the corporate ladder and away from the old homestead. Living in several different houses over time is the norm these days.

The amortization table (sometimes called the amortization scale) was created as a method for banks to lend money at the same time they were assured of a high rate of return on their investment. Although you'll pay the same monthly figure throughout the length of the loan, the allocation of those funds will change over time. Early on, the vast majority of your payment will be attributed only to the interest, not the principal; the lender gets its money back first. For example, let's say your monthly note is $2,000, but only $80 of that amount might go toward paying down your principal with the remaining $1,920 allocated to interest payments. After five or ten years, you may have paid your mortgage down by $5,000 or $10,000, but most of the payments have been on interest to your lender. Of course, eventually the tables are turned. (Pardon the pun, but it's true.) As time passes, more of your dollars are allocated toward the principal of your loan as fewer dollars are used to pay down the principal.

That's financing—the fuel that provides so many real estate opportunities in this country. The hundreds of thousands of homes bought each year aren't purchased outright by wealthy buyers who simply write a check and note "Paid in Full" on the bottom. These homes are bought with borrowed money (OPM) from the nation's largest lending institutions, money that is there for people like you. It's investment capital available in the form of mortgages.

HOW MUCH WILL IT COST?

The real question is, "How much can you afford?" It's a waste of time, effort, and hope to look at homes in the $200,000 to $250,000 range when you can only afford $75,000 to $150,000. It's important that you prequalify for a mortgage before you invest too much shoe leather, miles per gallon, and day dreaming in finding the perfect condo, co-op, or townhome.

Sit down with your Realtor or mortgage broker and determine what range you can realistically afford. This is no time to be shy or embarrassed about finances; everything will come out sooner or later. It's better to be fully informed up front before you waste a lot of time looking at the unobtainable. Lenders use a formula to determine what percentage of your income can be allocated toward purchasing a home. They also take a close look at your credit rating, which is why it's so important to take care of your credit. It's not something you can build or rebuild overnight.

Certainly, the more you earn, the more you have in savings or assets and the better financial picture you can paint. Two incomes are better than one. Still, regardless of what you think your situation may be, it's important to know with certainty. Get prequalified to make sure you're not overreaching.

The cost of a mortgage to the borrower depends on the state of the economy. As I'm writing this book, it's possible for the cost to be zero for many buyers because the mortgage market is so competitive. Many banks or lending institutions are absorbing costs that were previously passed along to borrowers; appraisals and other related fees are examples. This may or may not be the situation you face as your local market will dictate conditions in your area.

All journeys begin with a single, first step. When buying a new home, your first step must be financial prequalification. (After an interview assessment with a mortgage broker or lender, your income will be compared to the cost of ownership, payments of mortgage, utilities, assessments, and taxes. Your credit will be checked as well.) To do otherwise is to head in the wrong direction. The table in Figure 7.2 shows you what you may be able to afford based on the formulas used by lenders and mortgage brokers. When using the table, be sure to factor in any additional costs of association living to get an accurate picture.

FIXED AND ADJUSTABLE RATE MORTGAGES

A number of mortgages are on the market, but most likely the vast majority of you will be involved with only one of two: a fixed rate mortgage or an adjustable rate mortgage. A fixed rate mortgage is just that: the rate of interest you pay is fixed at the origination of the loan and remains at that figure until the loan is paid off. Regardless of the ups and downs of the economy, the rate remains the same, fixed in place. If interest rates go up, the borrower is protected. Of course, it's too bad if rates drop because the fixed rate can't follow that market trend.

An adjustable rate mortgage (ARM) adjusts on prescribed time frames and within certain limitations, which are important to know. An ARM allows you to borrow money at the lowest interest rate because the lender's money is tied up for only a short time at any given rate. As rates adjust upward over time, the lending institution will earn more money from the loan.

Adjustable rate mortgages may adjust every 90 days, every 6 months, or once a year. In some cases the loan may extend to 3- or 5-year

FIGURE 7.2 *Amortization Table*

Principal borrowed: $200,000.00
Annual payments: 12   **Total payments:** 360
Annual interest rate: 6.00%   **Periodic interest rate:** 0.5000%
Regular payment amount: $1,199.10
Note: the following numbers are estimates. See an amortization schedule for more accurate values.
Total repaid: $431,676.00
Total interest paid: $231,676.00

Payment	Principal	Interest	Cum Prin	Cum Int	Prin Bal
1	199.10	1000.00	199.10	1000.00	199800.90
2	200.10	999.00	399.20	1999.00	199600.80
3	201.10	998.00	600.30	2997.00	199399.70
4	202.10	997.00	802.40	3994.00	199197.60
5	203.11	995.99	1005.51	4989.99	198994.49
6	204.13	994.97	1209.64	5984.96	198790.36
7	205.15	993.95	1414.79	6978.91	198585.21
8	206.17	992.93	1620.96	7971.84	198379.04
9	207.20	991.90	1828.16	8963.74	198171.84
10	208.24	990.86	2036.40	9954.60	197963.60
11	209.28	989.82	2245.68	10944.42	197754.32
12	210.33	988.77	2456.01	11933.19	197543.99
13	211.38	987.72	2667.39	12920.91	197332.61
14	212.44	986.66	2879.83	13907.57	197120.17
15	213.50	985.60	3093.33	14893.17	196906.67
16	214.57	984.53	3307.90	15877.70	196692.10
17	215.64	983.46	3523.54	16861.16	196476.46
18	216.72	982.38	3740.26	17843.54	196259.74
19	217.80	981.30	3958.06	18824.84	196041.94
20	218.89	980.21	4176.95	19805.05	195823.05
21	219.98	979.12	4396.93	20784.17	195603.07
22	221.08	978.02	4618.01	21762.19	195381.99
23	222.19	976.91	4840.20	22739.10	195159.80
24	223.30	975.80	5063.50	23714.90	194936.50
25	224.42	974.68	5287.92	24689.58	194712.08
26	225.54	973.56	5513.46	25663.14	194486.54
27	226.67	972.43	5740.13	26635.57	194259.87
28	227.80	971.30	5967.93	27606.87	194032.07
29	228.94	970.16	6196.87	28577.03	193803.13
30	230.08	969.02	6426.95	29546.05	193573.05
31	231.23	967.87	6658.18	30513.92	193341.82
32	232.39	966.71	6890.57	31480.63	193109.43
33	233.55	965.55	7124.12	32446.18	192875.88
34	234.72	964.38	7358.84	33410.56	192641.16
35	235.89	963.21	7594.73	34373.77	192405.27
36	237.07	962.03	7831.80	35335.80	192168.20

Payment	Principal	Interest	Cum Prin	Cum Int	Prin Bal
37	238.26	960.84	8070.06	36296.64	191929.94
38	239.45	959.65	8309.51	37256.29	191690.49
39	240.65	958.45	8550.16	38214.74	191449.84
40	241.85	957.25	8792.01	39171.99	191207.99
41	243.06	956.04	9035.07	40128.03	190964.93
42	244.28	954.82	9279.35	41082.85	190720.65
43	245.50	953.60	9524.85	42036.45	190475.15
44	246.72	952.38	9771.57	42988.83	190228.43
45	247.96	951.14	10019.53	43939.97	189980.47
46	249.20	949.90	10268.73	44889.87	189731.27
47	250.44	948.66	10519.17	45838.53	189480.83
48	251.70	947.40	10770.87	46785.93	189229.13
49	252.95	946.15	11023.82	47732.08	188976.18
50	254.22	944.88	11278.04	48676.96	188721.96
51	255.49	943.61	11533.53	49620.57	188466.47
52	256.77	942.33	11790.30	50562.90	188209.70
53	258.05	941.05	12048.35	51503.95	187951.65
54	259.34	939.76	12307.69	52443.71	187692.31
55	260.64	938.46	12568.33	53382.17	187431.67
56	261.94	937.16	12830.27	54319.33	187169.73
57	263.25	935.85	13093.52	55255.18	186906.48
58	264.57	934.53	13358.09	56189.71	186641.91
59	265.89	933.21	13623.98	57122.92	186376.02
60	267.22	931.88	13891.20	58054.80	186108.80
61	268.56	930.54	14159.76	58985.34	185840.24
62	269.90	929.20	14429.66	59914.54	185570.34
63	271.25	927.85	14700.91	60842.39	185299.09
64	272.60	926.50	14973.51	61768.89	185026.49
65	273.97	925.13	15247.48	62694.02	184752.52
66	275.34	923.76	15522.82	63617.78	184477.18
67	276.71	922.39	15799.53	64540.17	184200.47
68	278.10	921.00	16077.63	65461.17	183922.37
69	279.49	919.61	16357.12	66380.78	183642.88
70	280.89	918.21	16638.01	67298.99	183361.99
71	282.29	916.81	16920.30	68215.80	183079.70
72	283.70	915.40	17204.00	69131.20	182796.00
73	285.12	913.98	17489.12	70045.18	182510.88
74	286.55	912.55	17775.67	70957.73	182224.33
75	287.98	911.12	18063.65	71868.85	181936.35
76	289.42	909.68	18353.07	72778.53	181646.93
77	290.87	908.23	18643.94	73686.76	181356.06
78	292.32	906.78	18936.26	74593.54	181063.74
79	293.78	905.32	19230.04	75498.86	180769.96
80	295.25	903.85	19525.29	76402.71	180474.71
81	296.73	902.37	19822.02	77305.08	180177.98
82	298.21	900.89	20120.23	78205.97	179879.77
83	299.70	899.40	20419.93	79105.37	179580.07
84	301.20	897.90	20721.13	80003.27	179278.87

Payment	Principal	Interest	Cum Prin	Cum Int	Prin Bal
85	302.71	896.39	21023.84	80899.66	178976.16
86	304.22	894.88	21328.06	81794.54	178671.94
87	305.74	893.36	21633.80	82687.90	178366.20
88	307.27	891.83	21941.07	83579.73	178058.93
89	308.81	890.29	22249.88	84470.02	177750.12
90	310.35	888.75	22560.23	85358.77	177439.77
91	311.90	887.20	22872.13	86245.97	177127.87
92	313.46	885.64	23185.59	87131.61	176814.41
93	315.03	884.07	23500.62	88015.68	176499.38
94	316.60	882.50	23817.22	88898.18	176182.78
95	318.19	880.91	24135.41	89779.09	175864.59
96	319.78	879.32	24455.19	90658.41	175544.81
97	321.38	877.72	24776.57	91536.13	175223.43
98	322.98	876.12	25099.55	92412.25	174900.45
99	324.60	874.50	25424.15	93286.75	174575.85
100	326.22	872.88	25750.37	94159.63	174249.63
101	327.85	871.25	26078.22	95030.88	173921.78
102	329.49	869.61	26407.71	95900.49	173592.29
103	331.14	867.96	26738.85	96768.45	173261.15
104	332.79	866.31	27071.64	97634.76	172928.36
105	334.46	864.64	27406.10	98499.40	172593.90
106	336.13	862.97	27742.23	99362.37	172257.77
107	337.81	861.29	28080.04	100223.66	171919.96
108	339.50	859.60	28419.54	101083.26	171580.46
109	341.20	857.90	28760.74	101941.16	171239.26
110	342.90	856.20	29103.64	102797.36	170896.36
111	344.62	854.48	29448.26	103651.84	170551.74
112	346.34	852.76	29794.60	104504.60	170205.40
113	348.07	851.03	30142.67	105355.63	169857.33
114	349.81	849.29	30492.48	106204.92	169507.52
115	351.56	847.54	30844.04	107052.46	169155.96
116	353.32	845.78	31197.36	107898.24	168802.64
117	355.09	844.01	31552.45	108742.25	168447.55
118	356.86	842.24	31909.31	109584.49	168090.69
119	358.65	840.45	32267.96	110424.94	167732.04
120	360.44	838.66	32628.40	111263.60	167371.60
121	362.24	836.86	32990.64	112100.46	167009.36
122	364.05	835.05	33354.69	112935.51	166645.31
123	365.87	833.23	33720.56	113768.74	166279.44
124	367.70	831.40	34088.26	114600.14	165911.74
125	369.54	829.56	34457.80	115429.70	165542.20
126	371.39	827.71	34829.19	116257.41	165170.81
127	373.25	825.85	35202.44	117083.26	164797.56
128	375.11	823.99	35577.55	117907.25	164422.45
129	376.99	822.11	35954.54	118729.36	164045.46
130	378.87	820.23	36333.41	119549.59	163666.59
131	380.77	818.33	36714.18	120367.92	163285.82
132	382.67	816.43	37096.85	121184.35	162903.15

Payment	Principal	Interest	Cum Prin	Cum Int	Prin Bal
133	384.58	814.52	37481.43	121998.87	162518.57
134	386.51	812.59	37867.94	122811.46	162132.06
135	388.44	810.66	38256.38	123622.12	161743.62
136	390.38	808.72	38646.76	124430.84	161353.24
137	392.33	806.77	39039.09	125237.61	160960.91
138	394.30	804.80	39433.39	126042.41	160566.61
139	396.27	802.83	39829.66	126845.24	160170.34
140	398.25	800.85	40227.91	127646.09	159772.09
141	400.24	798.86	40628.15	128444.95	159371.85
142	402.24	796.86	41030.39	129241.81	158969.61
143	404.25	794.85	41434.64	130036.66	158565.36
144	406.27	792.83	41840.91	130829.49	158159.09
145	408.30	790.80	42249.21	131620.29	157750.79
146	410.35	788.75	42659.56	132409.04	157340.44
147	412.40	786.70	43071.96	133195.74	156928.04
148	414.46	784.64	43486.42	133980.38	156513.58
149	416.53	782.57	43902.95	134762.95	156097.05
150	418.61	780.49	44321.56	135543.44	155678.44
151	420.71	778.39	44742.27	136321.83	155257.73
152	422.81	776.29	45165.08	137098.12	154834.92
153	424.93	774.17	45590.01	137872.29	154409.99
154	427.05	772.05	46017.06	138644.34	153982.94
155	429.19	769.91	46446.25	139414.25	153553.75
156	431.33	767.77	46877.58	140182.02	153122.42
157	433.49	765.61	47311.07	140947.63	152688.93
158	435.66	763.44	47746.73	141711.07	152253.27
159	437.83	761.27	48184.56	142472.34	151815.44
160	440.02	759.08	48624.58	143231.42	151375.42
161	442.22	756.88	49066.80	143988.30	150933.20
162	444.43	754.67	49511.23	144742.97	150488.77
163	446.66	752.44	49957.89	145495.41	150042.11
164	448.89	750.21	50406.78	146245.62	149593.22
165	451.13	747.97	50857.91	146993.59	149142.09
166	453.39	745.71	51311.30	147739.30	148688.70
167	455.66	743.44	51766.96	148482.74	148233.04
168	457.93	741.17	52224.89	149223.91	147775.11
169	460.22	738.88	52685.11	149962.79	147314.89
170	462.53	736.57	53147.64	150699.36	146852.36
171	464.84	734.26	53612.48	151433.62	146387.52
172	467.16	731.94	54079.64	152165.56	145920.36
173	469.50	729.60	54549.14	152895.16	145450.86
174	471.85	727.25	55020.99	153622.41	144979.01
175	474.20	724.90	55495.19	154347.31	144504.81
176	476.58	722.52	55971.77	155069.83	144028.23
177	478.96	720.14	56450.73	155789.97	143549.27
178	481.35	717.75	56932.08	156507.72	143067.92
179	483.76	715.34	57415.84	157223.06	142584.16
180	486.18	712.92	57902.02	157935.98	142097.98

Payment	Principal	Interest	Cum Prin	Cum Int	Prin Bal
181	488.61	710.49	58390.63	158646.47	141609.37
182	491.05	708.05	58881.68	159354.52	141118.32
183	493.51	705.59	59375.19	160060.11	140624.81
184	495.98	703.12	59871.17	160763.23	140128.83
185	498.46	700.64	60369.63	161463.87	139630.37
186	500.95	698.15	60870.58	162162.02	139129.42
187	503.45	695.65	61374.03	162857.67	138625.97
188	505.97	693.13	61880.00	163550.80	138120.00
189	508.50	690.60	62388.50	164241.40	137611.50
190	511.04	688.06	62899.54	164929.46	137100.46
191	513.60	685.50	63413.14	165614.96	136586.86
192	516.17	682.93	63929.31	166297.89	136070.69
193	518.75	680.35	64448.06	166978.24	135551.94
194	521.34	677.76	64969.40	167656.00	135030.60
195	523.95	675.15	65493.35	168331.15	134506.65
196	526.57	672.53	66019.92	169003.68	133980.08
197	529.20	669.90	66549.12	169673.58	133450.88
198	531.85	667.25	67080.97	170340.83	132919.03
199	534.50	664.60	67615.47	171005.43	132384.53
200	537.18	661.92	68152.65	171667.35	131847.35
201	539.86	659.24	68692.51	172326.59	131307.49
202	542.56	656.54	69235.07	172983.13	130764.93
203	545.28	653.82	69780.35	173636.95	130219.65
204	548.00	651.10	70328.35	174288.05	129671.65
205	550.74	648.36	70879.09	174936.41	129120.91
206	553.50	645.60	71432.59	175582.01	128567.41
207	556.26	642.84	71988.85	176224.85	128011.15
208	559.04	640.06	72547.89	176864.91	127452.11
209	561.84	637.26	73109.73	177502.17	126890.27
210	564.65	634.45	73674.38	178136.62	126325.62
211	567.47	631.63	74241.85	178768.25	125758.15
212	570.31	628.79	74812.16	179397.04	125187.84
213	573.16	625.94	75385.32	180022.98	124614.68
214	576.03	623.07	75961.35	180646.05	124038.65
215	578.91	620.19	76540.26	181266.24	123459.74
216	581.80	617.30	77122.06	181883.54	122877.94
217	584.71	614.39	77706.77	182497.93	122293.23
218	587.63	611.47	78294.40	183109.40	121705.60
219	590.57	608.53	78884.97	183717.93	121115.03
220	593.52	605.58	79478.49	184323.51	120521.51
221	596.49	602.61	80074.98	184926.12	119925.02
222	599.47	599.63	80674.45	185525.75	119325.55
223	602.47	596.63	81276.92	186122.38	118723.08
224	605.48	593.62	81882.40	186716.00	118117.60
225	608.51	590.59	82490.91	187306.59	117509.09
226	611.55	587.55	83102.46	187894.14	116897.54
227	614.61	584.49	83717.07	188478.63	116282.93
228	617.69	581.41	84334.76	189060.04	115665.24

Payment	Principal	Interest	Cum Prin	Cum Int	Prin Bal
229	620.77	578.33	84955.53	189638.37	115044.47
230	623.88	575.22	85579.41	190213.59	114420.59
231	627.00	572.10	86206.41	190785.69	113793.59
232	630.13	568.97	86836.54	191354.66	113163.46
233	633.28	565.82	87469.82	191920.48	112530.18
234	636.45	562.65	88106.27	192483.13	111893.73
235	639.63	559.47	88745.90	193042.60	111254.10
236	642.83	556.27	89388.73	193598.87	110611.27
237	646.04	553.06	90034.77	194151.93	109965.23
238	649.27	549.83	90684.04	194701.76	109315.96
239	652.52	546.58	91336.56	195248.34	108663.44
240	655.78	543.32	91992.34	195791.66	108007.66
241	659.06	540.04	92651.40	196331.70	107348.60
242	662.36	536.74	93313.76	196868.44	106686.24
243	665.67	533.43	93979.43	197401.87	106020.57
244	669.00	530.10	94648.43	197931.97	105351.57
245	672.34	526.76	95320.77	198458.73	104679.23
246	675.70	523.40	95996.47	198982.13	104003.53
247	679.08	520.02	96675.55	199502.15	103324.45
248	682.48	516.62	97358.03	200018.77	102641.97
249	685.89	513.21	98043.92	200531.98	101956.08
250	689.32	509.78	98733.24	201041.76	101266.76
251	692.77	506.33	99426.01	201548.09	100573.99
252	696.23	502.87	100122.24	202050.96	99877.76
253	699.71	499.39	100821.95	202550.35	99178.05
254	703.21	495.89	101525.16	203046.24	98474.84
255	706.73	492.37	102231.89	203538.61	97768.11
256	710.26	488.84	102942.15	204027.45	97057.85
257	713.81	485.29	103655.96	204512.74	96344.04
258	717.38	481.72	104373.34	204994.46	95626.66
259	720.97	478.13	105094.31	205472.59	94905.69
260	724.57	474.53	105818.88	205947.12	94181.12
261	728.19	470.91	106547.07	206418.03	93452.93
262	731.84	467.26	107278.91	206885.29	92721.09
263	735.49	463.61	108014.40	207348.90	91985.60
264	739.17	459.93	108753.57	207808.83	91246.43
265	742.87	456.23	109496.44	208265.06	90503.56
266	746.58	452.52	110243.02	208717.58	89756.98
267	750.32	448.78	110993.34	209166.36	89006.66
268	754.07	445.03	111747.41	209611.39	88252.59
269	757.84	441.26	112505.25	210052.65	87494.75
270	761.63	437.47	113266.88	210490.12	86733.12
271	765.43	433.67	114032.31	210923.79	85967.69
272	769.26	429.84	114801.57	211353.63	85198.43
273	773.11	425.99	115574.68	211779.62	84425.32
274	776.97	422.13	116351.65	212201.75	83648.35
275	780.86	418.24	117132.51	212619.99	82867.49
276	784.76	414.34	117917.27	213034.33	82082.73

Payment	Principal	Interest	Cum Prin	Cum Int	Prin Bal
277	788.69	410.41	118705.96	213444.74	81294.04
278	792.63	406.47	119498.59	213851.21	80501.41
279	796.59	402.51	120295.18	214253.72	79704.82
280	800.58	398.52	121095.76	214652.24	78904.24
281	804.58	394.52	121900.34	215046.76	78099.66
282	808.60	390.50	122708.94	215437.26	77291.06
283	812.64	386.46	123521.58	215823.72	76478.42
284	816.71	382.39	124338.29	216206.11	75661.71
285	820.79	378.31	125159.08	216584.42	74840.92
286	824.90	374.20	125983.98	216958.62	74016.02
287	829.02	370.08	126813.00	217328.70	73187.00
288	833.17	365.93	127646.17	217694.63	72353.83
289	837.33	361.77	128483.50	218056.40	71516.50
290	841.52	357.58	129325.02	218413.98	70674.98
291	845.73	353.37	130170.75	218767.35	69829.25
292	849.95	349.15	131020.70	219116.50	68979.30
293	854.20	344.90	131874.90	219461.40	68125.10
294	858.47	340.63	132733.37	219802.03	67266.63
295	862.77	336.33	133596.14	220138.36	66403.86
296	867.08	332.02	134463.22	220470.38	65536.78
297	871.42	327.68	135334.64	220798.06	64665.36
298	875.77	323.33	136210.41	221121.39	63789.59
299	880.15	318.95	137090.56	221440.34	62909.44
300	884.55	314.55	137975.11	221754.89	62024.89
301	888.98	310.12	138864.09	222065.01	61135.91
302	893.42	305.68	139757.51	222370.69	60242.49
303	897.89	301.21	140655.40	222671.90	59344.60
304	902.38	296.72	141557.78	222968.62	58442.22
305	906.89	292.21	142464.67	223260.83	57535.33
306	911.42	287.68	143376.09	223548.51	56623.91
307	915.98	283.12	144292.07	223831.63	55707.93
308	920.56	278.54	145212.63	224110.17	54787.37
309	925.16	273.94	146137.79	224384.11	53862.21
310	929.79	269.31	147067.58	224653.42	52932.42
311	934.44	264.66	148002.02	224918.08	51997.98
312	939.11	259.99	148941.13	225178.07	51058.87
313	943.81	255.29	149884.94	225433.36	50115.06
314	948.52	250.58	150833.46	225683.94	49166.54
315	953.27	245.83	151786.73	225929.77	48213.27
316	958.03	241.07	152744.76	226170.84	47255.24
317	962.82	236.28	153707.58	226407.12	46292.42
318	967.64	231.46	154675.22	226638.58	45324.78
319	972.48	226.62	155647.70	226865.20	44352.30
320	977.34	221.76	156625.04	227086.96	43374.96
321	982.23	216.87	157607.27	227303.83	42392.73
322	987.14	211.96	158594.41	227515.79	41405.59
323	992.07	207.03	159586.48	227722.82	40413.52
324	997.03	202.07	160583.51	227924.89	39416.49

Payment	Principal	Interest	Cum Prin	Cum Int	Prin Bal
325	1002.02	197.08	161585.53	228121.97	38414.47
326	1007.03	192.07	162592.56	228314.04	37407.44
327	1012.06	187.04	163604.62	228501.08	36395.38
328	1017.12	181.98	164621.74	228683.06	35378.26
329	1022.21	176.89	165643.95	228859.95	34356.05
330	1027.32	171.78	166671.27	229031.73	33328.73
331	1032.46	166.64	167703.73	229198.37	32296.27
332	1037.62	161.48	168741.35	229359.85	31258.65
333	1042.81	156.29	169784.16	229516.14	30215.84
334	1048.02	151.08	170832.18	229667.22	29167.82
335	1053.26	145.84	171885.44	229813.06	28114.56
336	1058.53	140.57	172943.97	229953.63	27056.03
337	1063.82	135.28	174007.79	230088.91	25992.21
338	1069.14	129.96	175076.93	230218.87	24923.07
339	1074.48	124.62	176151.41	230343.49	23848.59
340	1079.86	119.24	177231.27	230462.73	22768.73
341	1085.26	113.84	178316.53	230576.57	21683.47
342	1090.68	108.42	179407.21	230684.99	20592.79
343	1096.14	102.96	180503.35	230787.95	19496.65
344	1101.62	97.48	181604.97	230885.43	18395.03
345	1107.12	91.98	182712.09	230977.41	17287.91
346	1112.66	86.44	183824.75	231063.85	16175.25
347	1118.22	80.88	184942.97	231144.73	15057.03
348	1123.81	75.29	186066.78	231220.02	13933.22
349	1129.43	69.67	187196.21	231289.69	12803.79
350	1135.08	64.02	188331.29	231353.71	11668.71
351	1140.76	58.34	189472.05	231412.05	10527.95
352	1146.46	52.64	190618.51	231464.69	9381.49
353	1152.19	46.91	191770.70	231511.60	8229.30
354	1157.95	41.15	192928.65	231552.75	7071.35
355	1163.74	35.36	194092.39	231588.11	5907.61
356	1169.56	29.54	195261.95	231617.65	4738.05
357	1175.41	23.69	196437.36	231641.34	3562.64
358	1181.29	17.81	197618.65	231659.15	2381.35
359	1187.19	11.91	198805.84	231671.06	1194.16
360	*1194.16	5.97	200000.00	231677.03	0.00

*The final payment has been adjusted to account for payments having been rounded to the nearest cent.

terms, but the most popular time frame is 1 year. An ARM will usually have a cap, a limit, on the amount a loan can be adjusted within a year and is most commonly set at 2 percent a year. For example, if your loan is at 5 percent and interest rates suddenly skyrocket to 8 or 10 percent (or whatever), the amount your ARM can be adjusted upward can be no more than 7 percent—the limit set by the 2 percent cap.

In previous years, interest rates in this country have in fact skyrocketed upward at a phenomenally fast rate. Sometimes this was an induced situation to slow the economy and inflation by making money expensive to borrow. Historically, however, interest rates for housing have not varied significantly during the past century.

Many first-time buyers have a lot of fears and misconceptions about ARMs.

Some think that the rate can skyrocket at a moment's notice, forcing them into a financial panic as they try to come up with the extra cash to make the end-of-the-month house note. But it doesn't happen that way. Rules and regulations are in place governing how high and in what time frames rates can climb. I don't have any particular fears or qualms about adjustable rate mortgages. By keeping an interest rate low, a borrower can pay down more in his or her principal over a time period in which more cash is readily available.

Still, most people prefer the peace of mind found in a fixed rate mortgage. Some people seem to sleep better knowing that when they rise in the morning, their rates haven't. Peace of mind has a price tag, one that can be determined only by an individual borrower.

Most fixed rate mortgages are payable on a 15- or 30-year amortization scale. I recommend the 15-year term for people who want to pay off their mortgage as quickly as possible. Again, this is a matter of personal choice and preference. A 15-year mortgage has a higher rate, but your reduced monthly discretionary income is balanced by the fact that you'll be paying that note for fewer months—half as many to be precise.

Financing via mortgages is really the fire that fuels the real estate economy. I remember as a child that families in my neighborhood often held "mortgage burnings" on making their final payment. These were small parties, sometimes minifestivals, in celebration of completing a 30-year commitment to buying a home.

That we can deduct our home interest payments from our income tax in the United States is a terrific incentive to homebuyers. Still, I feel that it is better to pay down your principal and eliminate the interest payment or debt that you owe. I apply this rule across the board, not just to housing payments. Why pay for something when you can *pay off* something.

A mortgage is not a line of credit in which your interest rate or payments decrease monthly based on the amount of principal paid down.

The amortization table allows you to pay down your mortgage at a more accelerated rate provided the lender always receives the same percentage of interest. As previously noted, interest payments are higher at the front end than at the back.

HOW TO WORK WITH LENDING INSTITUTIONS

Earlier, I emphasized the importance of becoming prequalified as one of your first steps toward buying a condo, co-op, or townhome. Please do so and save yourself, your Realtor or broker, and numerous homesellers a lot of time and trouble. Know what you can buy before you start looking for it.

Shop around for the best financing, the best real estate professional, and the best personality fit between yourself and your agent. As you talk to multiple lenders, you'll discover that they're all pretty much the same. Again, shop around so you can cull the predatory lenders. It is unusual to find lenders who stray too far from the pack, but they do exist. Investigate very carefully people and companies offering loans that appear too good to be true; there's a good chance they require more stringent conditions on borrowers than do other lenders.

The market for borrowing money is like any other market. To be competitive you have to work within normal limits for your economy and geographic area, and according to local market conditions. Some predatory lenders charge as much as twice the norm for their market. Folks with poor credit may have to deal with them simply because their financial status eliminates them from consideration by most of the reputable lenders. If your credit is good, there's no reason for you to even consider working with a predatory lender.

Again, get out there, get to know a few lenders, and get yourself prequalified. If for no other reason, do it so you can see for yourself what I'm sharing in this book. Nothing beats direct, personal experience. Almost every lender will offer you the same dollar-for-dollar deal. If market rates decline, so will the rates charged by the lenders. If rates move upward, so will lender rates.

Then why not just take the first deal from the first lender? I think you should shop around for the dealer as well as the deal. Different real estate professionals have different skills, levels of experience, willingness to go the extra mile, people skills, and other qualifications. I believe it's important to find someone you like, trust, and believe has your best interests at heart. They're out there, lots of 'em. You just have to do a bit of looking and interviewing to find them. Believe me, the effort is well worth it.

Some lenders have different floor and ceiling rates. A floor rate is a rate that cannot drop below a set limit. Conversely, a ceiling rate cannot climb above a certain rate. Although rates *may* vary slightly, you'll generally find the same financial arrangement across the board with reputable lenders.

I learned a valuable lesson many years ago. Borrowing money for mortgages is generally much easier when the lending institution is near the property for which you want the mortgage. Some bankers say they like to be able to look out the window and see the property before they make the loan. Working locally has several advantages. Your local lender, for example, understands your market. A fact, figure, or situation that might alarm a distant lender could be considered no problem at all to a local lender who has the "inside scoop" on the situation. Locals have a history in the community and a sense of history about the community—surprisingly valuable when seeking a mortgage.

MEET YOUR NEW LENDER

The title of this section isn't the name of a new network game show or the latest in reality programming. You might acquire a mortgage from one lending institution only to discover later on that you are making payments to another, because lending institutions often sell mortgage notes to other institutions, which then collect the money from borrowers and pay off the institution originating the loan. That original bank has then replenished capital that it can lend out to create more profits.

I acquired my first condo in 1982, a time when I wasn't 100 percent sure of the mortgage process. Rates were extremely high, and I considered myself lucky to get a 13 percent interest rate. (How times have changed!) My attorney recommended that we ask the lender if it would finance my acquisition from the seller, and that's how I got my first mortgage. I was lucky. The mortgage was held by a community bank, and the loan committee wanted to keep the loan in-house. I qualified, and they were willing to work with me to make sure the mortgage went through without a hitch. Considering how things are in today's market, it was an interesting experience to have the loan stay with the original lender.

These days community banks aren't as easy to find, but they're still out there. The huge megabanks haven't gobbled them all up, so it's worth the effort to find community banks to see if you can work out a favorable mortgage. Even if you don't find the perfect community lender, many lenders with many different kinds of deals are out there. You may even discover that the institution with which you prequalify might turn out to be the lender on your acquisition.

A few years after my purchase of that first condo, rates dropped to a (then) phenomenal low of 10 percent. I approached a local lender for refinancing, my main purpose being to reduce my monthly payment. The appraisal report shocked me. In just two years my condo was worth less than what I had paid for it, and the bank wouldn't refinance because of the property's diminished value.

More than shocked, I was furious. I knew something was wrong and I made it my business to find out what it was. I drove around the neighborhood with the real estate appraiser to get a first-hand look at comparable sales. We discovered that although I lived in a contemporary condo built during the 1960s, the buildings that were compared with mine were vintage properties with smaller room sizes, no air-conditioning, and lacking other modern conveniences and features. The comparisons were patently unfair.

I presented the proper comparables to the lender, who recognized that the appraisal was defective, and gave my material to the appraiser. *Beware of a defective appraisal.* They are more common than one would think. My refinancing took place, later than expected, yet I prevailed.

The lesson is to take control when control is necessary.

COMING TO TERMS WITH MORTGAGES

Here are a few common terms you'll need to know when applying for a mortgage.

The *annual percentage rate* (APR) is the rate of interest on a loan per year. Disclosure is mandatory because of the Truth-in-Lending Act (15

U.S.C.A. §§1601 et seq.), and includes the interest rate, points, broker fees, and other credit charges, all of which are expressed as a yearly rate.

The *closing* is the act of transferring a property from the seller to the buyer according to the terms of a sales contract. Closing is also used to refer to the actual meeting at which the transfer takes place.

Closing costs include a number of fees and charges related to the closing that are paid by the seller and the buyer. These include broker's fees, lender's discount fees, title insurance premium, application fees, title examination, abstract of title, title insurance, deed recording fees, loan prepayment penalty, inspection/appraisal fees, attorney fees, credit report fees, and notary fees.

Conventional loans are mortgage loans that are not backed by a government agency such as the Federal Housing Administration (FHA), the Veterans Administration (VA), or other government bodies.

When a third party holds money (or documents) before the closing, the money is said to be in *escrow*. A homeowner may also pay money into a lender-held escrow account for taxes and insurance.

The *interest rate* is the cost to you of acquiring a loan expressed as a percentage. A fixed rate remains constant throughout the life of the loan. An adjustable rate fluctuates up or down according to market conditions.

Loan origination fees are lender charges, usually expressed as a percentage of the loan, for handling the loan.

A written agreement guaranteeing a specific rate for the buyer is called a *lock-in*. There is usually a time limit on a lock-in, such as 30, 60, or 90 days.

A *mortgage* is a written agreement between borrower and lender whereby the lender gains the right to take possession of the property should the owner default on the loan.

The financial difference between the lowest available loan cost and the amount that the borrower actually agrees on is called an *overage*. The loan officers or brokers who are allowed to keep some or all of this difference have another word for it—*profit*.

Points are fees paid to a lender or broker. Usually 1 percent of the principal loan amount equals one point. Generally, the more points you pay, the lower your interest rate. Whenever you're talking points, be sure to request they be stated in dollar figures. It's easy to forget that three points may represent a fee of several thousand dollars or more.

Thrift institution is just another way of saying bank or savings and loan.

Money talks and when you find, acquire, and put money to work buying your new home, you'll feel like the talk of the town.

8

FINDING THE RIGHT LOCATION

"Ask, and it shall be given to you; seek and ye shall find; knock, and it shall be opened unto you."

Matthew 7:7

One of the first things prospective homebuyers examine—and examine with that proverbial fine-tooth comb—is the environment in which they might live. That is to say, they check out the neighborhood. If you ask ten people what they are looking for in a neighborhood, you'll get ten different answers. Certainly, there will be overlapping desires and concerns, but the emphasis varies from person to person, couple to couple, and family to family. Many factors are involved. Among them are these:

- Age
- Income
- Size of, or lack of, immediate family
- Proximity to employment
- Schools
- Cultural opportunities
- Recreational outlets
- Religion
- The emotional "feel" of the neighborhood

All factors are important, but heading the list must be your financial status. As I've noted previously, it's futile to look at ultraluxury properties when you're a first-time buyer. Champagne is nice, but it's not on the menu with a beer budget. A family's financial status changes throughout life, and the change is generally for the better. The first-time buyer becomes a second-time buyer and so on, each time moving up to bigger, better, and more luxurious properties, so don't give up or think small. Owners keep on building those ultraluxury properties because they believe someone will be available to purchase them. One day you too might be in the market.

The search for a good neighborhood begins with the search for the right condo, co-op, or townhome. I recommend that you begin by casting a wide net. Broaden your search to include many areas, not just the dream neighborhood you've seen advertised in the classifieds. Too often buyers start out thinking they're living on that champagne budget, and their dreams are dashed early because they're looking for properties that they just can't afford at the moment. Think beyond the right home; consider different neighborhoods, suburbs, and even different cities and towns. Opportunity is everywhere, but you have to look for it.

Be realistic and honest with yourself and your Realtor. Look at areas you may not have considered when you first started looking. Express to your real estate agent your willingness to look at any reasonable property. Help the agent out with positive feedback after every visit. Take a few moments to go over what you liked and what you didn't like about the property, the neighborhood, and any other important factors. Honest feedback helps the Realtor weed out a lot of properties and saves both of you a lot of time and energy. Work with your Realtor, and if you're on a beer budget, say so.

Hey, I'm from Chicago. I like beer!

Speaking of Chicago, the city and its suburbs offer a look at much of what you can expect to find, in a general way, in different parts of the country. The Chicago area has a good mix of downtown, suburban, and outlying properties available for purchase. Many first-time buyers start their search near the lake where they find lake views, jogging tracks, tennis courts, golf courses, city amenities, and a public park system that I believe is the finest in the country. Many cities and towns have such desirable areas, even if they aren't on the scale offered by Chicago.

For excellent reasons other people prefer a suburban lifestyle, finding too much hustle and bustle in the heart of the city. The suburbs offer many of the city's advantages without the perceived disadvantages of a big city.

A key factor in selecting a condo, co-op, or townhome in the suburbs is proximity to your place of employment or places of employment if both you and your spouse work. I know that the only thing we really have in this world is time, so we'd best make the best of it while we can. Most folks want a home within a reasonable driving distance of their workplace. A two-hour commute to and from work eats up four hours a day—half a standard workday. I see this a lot and find it sad when a family can't really be a family because one or more of the parents are investing what should be quality time in driving time. Add to that the extra cost of travel and the frustrations associated with rush-hour traffic, and I think you'll agree that the quality of your lifestyle could be taking a major hit if your home is too far from your work. Is the new dwelling worth it? Can't you find quality housing a bit closer to your place of work?

Many people willingly settle for a property that isn't 100 percent what they want because its proximity to work allows them more time with friends and family. This is, of course, a judgment call, but I recommend that you invest a considerable amount of time in serious thought before you make the call. All we really do have is time, and the neighborhood you choose will have a significant impact on whether that time is merely used or is invested in building a great life.

Families with kids or couples planning on kids will want to consider the school system, which for many people actually defines a neighborhood. Is it a good school in a good system? Is it nearby or will you need to find a carpool? What's its record for academic excellence? Are there problems with gangs or drugs? What type of extracurricular activities are available? Is input from parents encouraged or discouraged? These questions and many others are important considerations.

Religion is another factor in selecting a neighborhood because many neighborhoods, especially older ones, have often been defined by the religion of its inhabitants. Chicago, for example, became the hub city of the central United States more than a 100 years ago, a position it still occupies. Many of the waves of immigrants that have contributed so much to our nation's history and culture washed up on our Lake Michigan shores. People arrived here from Europe, Central Europe, Latin America, and many other parts of the world. Their backgrounds were incredibly diverse, but all shared at least one factor in common: the Catholic Church.

If you visit the many Catholic Churches in Chicago, you'll notice they cross many neighborhood lines, bringing together German, Polish, Irish, Mexican, and many other Catholics into a religious community. That's a rich mix of people, cultures, and histories for which the city is far better off. If you're Catholic, Jewish, Buddhist, Southern Baptist, Muslim, Wiccan, or belong to some other religion or belief system, you might want to consider the advantages of locating within a neighborhood of fellow believers. Again, that's a judgment call, but it is certainly a factor you'll want to consider.

Price, schools, proximity to work, religious affiliations, and other elements of a good lifestyle are important considerations for the immediate future, but think further down the road also. How will the neighborhood meet your needs when your children are ready for high school or when they move on to college and then out on their own? Are the features that attract you today going to be equally attractive when it's just you and your spouse living in the neighborhood? Is housing in the neighborhood appreciating in value? Can you earn enough from the sale of your condo, co-op, or townhome to move up into a bigger and better one?

Always buy property with an eye to the future. What will happen to the property value, the neighborhood, the city, or suburb within the next decade or two? You don't want to invest in a neighborhood on the decline. Not only will the value of your property likely diminish, but so will the quality of your lifestyle. Still, don't be fooled by outward appearances pro or con. Many a neighborhood that appears to be on the skids may actually be inhabited by active, aggressive, and committed community activists. What looks at first to be a rough area could be one in transition. People could be busy smoothing things out, and the community may be on its way to becoming a great place to live and raise a family. Don't be fooled either way by first appearances. Do your homework. Ask questions. Look around. Meet the potential neighbors. Then, and only then, make your final decision.

The bottom line is simple: Open yourself up to all opportunities; cast that net widely on the waters. Broaden your search initially and then begin to narrow your focus.

RESEARCH THE NEIGHBORHOOD TREND

An associate of mine in the desert Southwest is an avid hiker. Less than ten years ago, he could drive from his city though a smaller city and onto a highway winding through the desert mountains. He would take a rough, dusty "washboard" road off the highway to one of his favorite trailheads many miles from civilization. Today that drive through the desert is also a drive past shopping centers, several upscale housing developments and gated communities, a trendy golf course, a motel, and an apparently never-ending area of new construction. That dusty road is now paved, splitting apart a housing development and a brand-new school. He laments the final indignity—the state has put in landscaped toilets at the trailhead.

Encroaching civilization means land development and land redevelopment. New neighborhoods in America are sprouting like wildflowers after a desert rain. Raw land becomes a subdivision that attracts shopping centers, schools, and other city amenities. Farmlands become upscale communities. Suburbs, cities, and even industrial properties are continually being reinvented as the needs of the population change. So long as people need good housing and so long as real estate developers are meeting their needs, there will always be innovations in living trends and neighborhood trends.

Fifteen years ago, the movement of large numbers of people back into downtown areas of the country would have been unthinkable. But in the early 1990s, the suburban movement of earlier decades started to reverse itself. Developers (and renters and buyers) began to see that many of the abandoned or ill-used Class C buildings in downtown areas could be turned into highly desirable, highly profitable residential properties. I believe that you'll find this trend in any American city with a downtown offering basic amenities and nightlife.

The movement back to the cities occurred at the same time another trend began emerging. A lot of people started to sell their suburban properties and were looking for new places to live for many reasons. A lot of parents, for example, had sent their kids off to college and now suddenly found themselves with a considerable amount of unused, yet costly, space in the old homestead. Others wanted a simpler lifestyle without yard work, home repairs, and continual upkeep. Still others just missed a bit of the "hustle and bustle" of the city they'd left many years before.

These two trends—a movement back to the cities and forgoing the suburban lifestyle—found common ground in new residential properties within the cities. A merger of interests became inevitable. The trend to city life even extended into old industrial parks on the borders of the city. Nothing ever really goes to waste in nature. In real estate that change may take some time, but even rusted ruins (certainly the land beneath them) have a way of bouncing back, evolving, and becoming something entirely new and valuable.

I travel across the United States all the time, and I'm always seeing properties that at one time were unpopular and underused now becoming thriving residential communities. This is an exciting change in an era of exciting change. I hope you find buying your condo, co-op, or townhome as thrilling as I have. Considering the quantity of properties out there and the availability of financing to acquire them, I believe you will.

The United States has a vast inventory of land and buildings. Because we are constantly changing and have constantly changing living needs, we will always be tearing down the old to build the new. A good example is Celebration, Florida, a true mixed-use community consisting of townhomes, condominiums, single-family dwellings, and even rental properties. The city, designed for a population of 20,000 residents, is an interesting mix of the old and the new. The community is designed to look like an old-fashioned, 19th century American town, yet each house is wired with the latest fiber-optic technology. When complete, the project will have a downtown, public school, post office, town hall, 18-hole golf course, tennis courts, nature trails, a health center, a 1-million-square-foot business park, and a downtown lake. Apartment prices are slated to start at $650; home prices will range from $127,000 to $750,000.

Opinions are mixed whether a 19th century-style community can survive the realities of the 20th century. No one really knows, but the savvy Disney organization is betting $2.5 billion that it can. Of course, everything is a gamble. The exciting fact is that in America so many gambles pay off.

Celebration is just one of many exciting events in real estate. Some of the new communities going up throughout the country might not be as ambitious as Celebration, but nonetheless communities are going up. Old neighborhoods are finding new life in new homes and new families. Condos, co-ops, and townhomes are a big part of that movement.

One of those communities might be just right for you.

HOW TO FIND THE RIGHT PROPERTY

As I have written in numerous books, and as I have said in many seminars, the right house for you depends on a number of factors. These factors may change with age, income levels, the size of your family, the local economy, your physical needs, your aesthetic needs, and so on. To find the right house at any one time you have to carefully examine, weigh, and evaluate all of the following questions:

- How well will your furniture match the home you want to acquire?
- Are you divorced and moving into a smaller dwelling requiring fewer pieces?
- Do you want your kids in the best possible school system?
- Can you really afford the homes you're walking through?
- What will the neighborhood be like in a few years? In a decade or more?
- Have you looked around enough?

That last question is key. The only way to find the right condo, co-op, or townhome is to look, look some more, and then keep on looking. For some people this is a piece of cake; they enjoy the process so much it's almost a game; decisions come fast and easily. Others take a more emotional approach, looking for the home with just the right feel, which is hard to quantify, especially for an objective Realtor, but it's something buyers tend to notice instinctively. Still others are so logical that *Star Trek's* Mr. Spock would be proud of their unemotional approach.

The real key is to find, and work closely with, a good real estate professional, someone who knows the business, knows the community, and will invest the time to know you and your needs. The support system provided by your friends and family can be invaluable. Not only can these people network in the community for you, they can offer objective advice and opinions when your enthusiasm for a property might be overwhelming your thinking processes.

People are often overwhelmed by the number of condos, co-ops, and townhomes they tour. Instead of becoming easier with each tour, the final decision becomes more and more difficult. Eventually, some people reach a saturation point, literally freeze up and can't make a decision. A simple and effective measure can avoid that.

Instead of searching directly for the perfect home, start by eliminating the ones that don't measure up. You have to make sure you're looking at a lot of properties to make this process work, but you should be doing that anyway. When a neighborhood doesn't feel right, cross the property off your list. If you really don't like the style, "X" it out. If it's too small, too large, or poorly laid out, then forget it. You have lots of homes left to see.

You might have to resist some pressure from your Realtor or your network of friends and family. Yes, always listen to their opinions, but make up your own mind. If you're not completely happy with a dwelling during a walk-through, chances are good that you won't be very happy living there. The first dwelling you cross off the list will be the most challenging, because you'll be excited and full of energy and you'll want to locate that dream home right off the bat. Resist temptation. Evaluate everything with a cold and calculating eye, and if a place doesn't measure up, move on. Something better is (literally) right around the corner.

Eventually, you'll winnow down your long list of "possibles" to a short list of "probables." Making the right decision on the right property is much simpler and easier at that point. Again, the trick isn't to locate the perfect home immediately; it's to use the process of elimination so that at some point the choice becomes obvious. In fact, at some point you won't have to make a choice at all. You'll know it when you get there.

The right property is out there and you can find it. Do your research. Finish your homework. Take the walk-throughs. Make the deal and, as Mr. Spock would say, "Live long and prosper."

HOW TO EVALUATE PROPERTY

Carefully. That's how you evaluate property. It's truly a team effort involving yourself, your Realtor, attorney, inspector, family, and friends. Get everyone involved. Each person has his or her own expertise, and each can add a valuable perspective to the overall decision to purchase the property or to move on to something better.

First on your list of consultants is your Realtor. Realtors know the market. They know the properties, the owners, and the managers and how well the properties have been maintained. If they lack such information, they're "wired in" and can acquire it faster and with more accuracy than the average buyer. Realtors are also aware of trends, many of them subtle or not yet publicly known, and can guide your buying decision so that you don't regret the purchase a year or two down the road. A neighborhood that has bottomed out and appears to be a disaster area may actually be headed back up and could soon be a wonderful place to live. An apparently ideal neighborhood could just as easily be sliding backwards. Realtors are aware of such trends and can provide fair, objective input into your decision.

Inspectors are also invaluable. They are often just as aware, or even more aware, than Realtors are of the quality of construction in a neighborhood, development, or even a particular structure. They know if a builder or developer has a reputation for excellent or shoddy work. They know which neighborhoods have a reputation for recurring repair and maintenance work. They can recognize serious problems where you and I might see only superficial opportunity. A home inspector is an invaluable member of your team, so do not under any circumstances pass up his or her expertise.

From time to time I encounter a property that was poorly built or poorly maintained, yet the property is on the market, serious buyers are looking at it, and someone sooner or later will become the "proud new owner." Sadly, he or she becomes the proud new owner of a real pain in the you-know-what. This trouble takes the form of serious financial burdens, obligations, and inconvenience. Maintaining and repairing a property can be a nightmare if the structure isn't sound.

A condo, co-op, or townhome may be presented to you as a pristine, trouble-free dream home. You may also get a visit from the tooth fairy, win the lottery, discover a cure for the common cold, and learn to fly by flapping your arms. Don't get me wrong. There are more good properties out there than bad ones, but you have to make the investment in time, money, and energy to weed out the bad from the good. To neglect this essential responsibility is to tie yourself to a financial burden for many years to come. Expensive, inconvenient, and time-consuming problems could include excessive settling, a bad foundation, a poorly constructed roof, inefficient heating and cooling systems, unsafe electrical wiring, ancient plumbing, and many other problems. Most of these nightmares can be avoided if you make sure the property is fully inspected. Even if you elect to purchase the property anyway, you can negotiate with the owner for a lower price and/or to have the problems corrected before you take possession.

"Look before you leap" is especially applicable in real estate. By all means leap, but always make sure you're headed for a soft landing.

BUT IS THIS PROPERTY RIGHT FOR ME?

That depends. The yes or no answer depends on a large number of variables, many of them personal. What's right for John Doe isn't necessarily right for Richard Roe, Mrs. Roe, and all the little Roes. Still, so many good and available properties are out there that my attitude has always been that you really have to work hard to buy a property that *isn't* right.

But let's take the opposite tack and say that the property you've just purchased hasn't turned out to be the dream house you envisioned. What's the worst-case scenario? The worst case is that you'd want to sell it quickly and get out from under the investment. In most cases you'd sell it for what you paid, or you might even earn a little return on your money. Should something like this happen, take heart. One, if you've made a mistake, you'll know it pretty soon and can quickly begin taking steps to correct the situation. Two, real estate markets don't change that rapidly. The chances of taking a major loss are very slim.

Let's assume the very worst of the worst-case scenarios. You've made a mistake and want to sell, but the market is down so you'll have to take a loss. I'm not saying that such a situation is good, but it is still preferable to living in a home that's not right for you; if you can't stand the house, you certainly don't need to be *in* the house. I'd prefer to take the hit and get the misery behind me than to continue living in a home that made me unhappy every time I walked through the front door. There's a lot to be said for a good quality of life.

Keep in mind that in the vast majority of real estate purchases, the property turns out to be the right property. Unless you have a sudden and unexpected lifestyle change or unless you discover something bad that you missed during the evaluation phase, chances are you needn't worry about the property being right. Trust your instincts. Talk to the professionals. Get opinions from friends and family. Also, take courage from the following comments.

I have lived in and owned three residential properties in my life. The first was a condo that I knew immediately on seeing was the right home for me. I had looked around a good bit and had consulted my network of professionals, friends, and family. The place had a lot going for it; it was affordable and much larger than I believed I could afford. Even though at that time I knew next to nothing about real estate and real estate contracts, I was excited as a kid at Christmas when I made the purchase. I just "knew" the property would work out. My instinct was 100 percent on target.

I had the same feeling when I purchased my next two residential properties. With each purchase I did my homework, listened to the advice of my network, and trusted my instinct. Each time, I selected the property that was right for me. If you don't already know, you'll eventually realize that every ten years we become a different person. The condo you need at age 25 won't meet your family's needs at age 35 nor will it fulfill your needs and desires when you approach retirement age. Things change. Life moves on. Fortunately, the right condo, co-op, or townhome will always be available. Just ask around, knock on the door, and open yourself up to the opportunity.

9

I'VE FOUND WHAT I LIKE—NOW WHAT?

*"Have confidence that if you have done a little thing well,
you can do a bigger thing well, too."*

Joseph Storey

I want you to have confidence in your ability to find, negotiate for, purchase, live in, enjoy, and sell a terrific condominium, co-op, or townhome. And that you can do so again and again throughout your life if you so choose. I have confidence in you because I have been where you are and have experienced what you are experiencing. *You can achieve more than you believe because you know more than you think you know.*

You have read the previous chapters in this book. You've studied the information and have taken it to heart. You've also looked around. You've seen what you like and what you don't like. You know all the steps and techniques involved. Now what?

Now you put it all together. In this chapter I show you how to maneuver through the following six key "now what" areas:

1. Negotiations
2. Inspections
3. Association materials
4. Attorney approval
5. Financing
6. Rental or sale contingency

Study the material, take it to heart, and be confident. You've found what you like. Now go get it.

YOU MUST PLAY THE NEGOTIATIONS GAME

I think *game* is a word tossed about too freely in business, especially when it's used to describe such an important facet of real estate as negotiations. Nonetheless, you will certainly hear the term *game* applied to the word *negotiations*. Just be sure that you realize this game is one of the most serious experiences you will ever have.

So much of the real estate game is standardized these days. Real estate forms, multilist formats, and legal descriptions are virtually identical from San Diego to Savannah, and much of your real estate contract is universally accepted boilerplate. The negotiation phase of real estate acquisition is one of the few areas left where the participants can actually bargain. Some love the competition and enjoy the strategy and tactics of the so-called game. Others fear the process and just want to get through what they perceive as a tortuous experience. Whichever side you come down on is irrelevant. If you are to acquire the property you've found at the most favorable arrangement possible, you have to learn to play this game and to play it to win. I assure you, the other side will be playing for keeps.

The seller always asks a price that leaves room for negotiation. This is a standard part of the process, and everyone knows it. The seller usually has a high and a low figure in mind. He or she and the Realtor would love to get $250,000 for the condo but will, with a little negotiation, be happy to settle for $225,000. Their job is to get you, the buyer, to pay the full amount or as close to that amount as they can get. Your job is to get to the lower figure or as close to it as you can. Again, this is a serious matter. Each "point" scored in the game means a gain or loss of tens of thousands of dollars over time.

Learn from the Experts

Buying and selling is so standardized in the United States that most Americans have lost the art of negotiation. Many of us don't even realize that it can still be done. Things are different in other countries where negotiation is an art, a skill, and a basic way of conducting business. Even the owners of small shops and stands in the marketplace are experts. We could and should learn from them.

I took a trip to Mexico while preparing this book and observed the process firsthand. No self-respecting shop owner in any store or marketplace expects a customer to pay "sticker price." In fact, the owner would be surprised by anyone who did; of course, the owner would gladly accept your money if you insisted.

Just as in real estate, the purchase price in the shop or at the stand includes room for negotiation. I've observed skilled sellers and equally skilled buyers negotiate for a considerable time over a valuable article. Sometimes the buyer will even walk away from the deal only to return later to try for a better price. Usually by the end of the day, the sale is complete and both parties are satisfied with a win-win situation. It's okay to feel that you have done a little bit better in the bargaining than the other fellow; ideally, he feels the same way.

My son, who has grown up in the nonbargaining atmosphere of the American city, was a bit shocked to see negotiation taking place on normal commodities. You just don't do that down at the mall. At first he was upset that I'd offer a merchant less, often far less, than the price on the ticket or sticker. He even felt I was trying to cheat the poor merchant, so I had to explain that the game was played a bit differently in other parts of the world. I'm still not sure he grasps the concept that most vendors consider it an insult if you do not attempt to negotiate. If he decides to follow in my footsteps and enter the world of real estate, it's a skill he'll have to develop.

In the early 1970s, I spent time in Israel and found the exact same process at work with the Arab merchants in the marketplaces. Negotiation over the price of coats, rugs, lamps, pipes, or whatever was an exciting game to be played, and a game enjoyed fully by both sides. We would walk into an Arab market in the old city of Jerusalem, sit on a pile of rugs, and drink coffee; after an hour or so, we would begin to haggle over the price of the item we were acquiring at the time. Negotiation is part of the system, and it is important for buyer and seller to respect it so that the system continues working.

Apply Your Skills to a Bigger Marketplace

For most of us the biggest marketplace we'll ever shop is the real estate market. You can apply the same negotiating skills used in the shops and stands of other countries to purchase real estate in this country. Buying an automobile and buying real estate are the only two major areas in this country where we can still negotiate a significantly better price.

When you're buying your first condo, co-op, or townhome, your Realtor has the advantage. If the seller is asking $250,000, you want to find out what the Realtor believes is the seller's lowest price. But that's not all. You also want to develop a strategy that includes a beginning point—the first low price you'll offer. Also included is an exit strategy, the highest price you are willing to pay before walking away from the deal. The offers, counteroffers, and wheeling and dealing that occur between the beginning point and the exit strategy are merely the application of strategy and tactics—all part of the game.

As a rule of thumb, negotiation works within approximately 10 percent of the asking price. I can hear the questions forming in your minds now: "If everyone knows that and if everyone plays by the same rules, why don't we just split the difference and cut out all those time-consuming negotiations?" The answer is simple: that's not how the system works. Again, we're talking tens of thousands of dollars. Add in interest payments over time and you're talking about a lot of tens of thousands of dollars. The stakes are serious, and each side wants to make the best deal possible. This is the way it is, so you had better accept it. The only way you can take serious negotiation out of the picture is to pay more than you have to for your property.

The 10 percent rule doesn't apply across the board because local and regional economies have an effect. In hot markets, in cities with strong employment, and in areas attracting a lot of people, you may find properties selling at, or even above, the listing price. If there's a lot of competition for a condo listed for $250,000, hopeful buyers could easily up the ante. You can sometimes find properties that are actually underpriced in some markets, too. In those cases, paying the asking price or a price very close to it still earns you a real value and can be considered a bargain.

In most cases you'll encounter sellers who want, and expect, to negotiate. "Let the games begin!" When you prepare to make your first offer below the asking price, also prepare a few items I call "gimmes." These are negotiating items that really aren't important to you, but they're items you can easily give up during the negotiations. Get the point? The seller believes he or she has negotiated you down by refusing to accept your conditions. You eventually drop the demands, and the buyer has a sense of satisfaction at winning something in the negotiation. In point of fact, from your perspective the seller hasn't won anything of value at all.

I always want to win at negotiations, but I realize the value of always creating a win-win situation. The idea of beating someone down just because I can is unacceptable behavior to me. In addition to the basic morality of the situation, remember that you'll probably be buying and selling real estate in that market several times over the years. You'll want and need allies down the road, not enemies out to seek revenge or people speaking ill of your business ethics. Buyer, seller, Realtor, broker, and anyone else involved in the process should walk away feeling satisfied.

This Is Where the Fun Begins

The first step in buying your condo, co-op, or townhome is the contract, and that's where the fun really begins. Your Realtor will have a standard contract available, and again you won't find too much variation from Miami to Moose Jaw, from Bakersfield to Boston, or Corpus Christi to Casper. The contract provides a number of standard items, including these:

- Address
- Unit number
- City
- State
- Offering price
- Amount of earnest money
- Increased amount of earnest money on seller's acceptance
- Contingency clause for financing
- Contingency clause for inspection

- Amount of the assessments you'll be expected to pay
- Other items the seller will deliver as personal property, such as stove, refrigerator, microwave oven, television antenna, gardening, plantings, and so on
- A specific date by which the seller must accept or reject the contract

Your Realtor will present the contract to the seller or the seller's real estate agent. This is your offer. As part of the negotiating process, you will then receive a counteroffer from the seller, usually lower than the asking price but higher than your first offer. You respond with another counteroffer of your own. The process is something like a Ping-Pong game. You hit the ball to their side and they hit it back to you. In the final move of the game, one side will make the final move, and that's where the ball lands.

At some point you have to decide if the terms and conditions the seller has imposed or requested are acceptable. The seller may change your financing terms, request more earnest money, ask that you waive an inspection, or request some other change. Most sellers realize that the conventionality of offers must include your financing and inspection contingencies, so they typically won't ask you to make those changes.

If the final form of the contract is acceptable and you agree to it, congratulations. You have your first deal.

INSPECTIONS: NOW THAT YOU'VE BOUGHT IT, LOOK AT IT

Of course, you've looked at your new property, but now you need, and have the right to, another, far more in-depth look. Your contract gives you the right to have a professional inspection of the property to make sure that your new property is as sound as you have been led to believe. The contract will state a time frame within which you must make your inspections. The actual amount of time may vary according to your Realtor's suggestions or your own time frame, but generally the mortgage contingency runs 45 days, attorney approval requires 5 business days, and the inspections occur within 5 to 10 business days after acceptance of the contract.

Find a good home inspector. By *good* I don't mean a martinet or self-important blowhard who is proud of being a deal breaker. I do mean a professional who will provide a thorough and honest inspection. Look for someone your Realtor has worked with successfully. A good inspector can provide peace of mind by giving your new property a clean bill of health. If there are problem areas or potential problem areas that should be addressed before you acquire the unit, a good inspector will find them, and you can accept the situation or begin negotiations for the seller to make repairs.

Everyone comes to the negotiating table with his or her own subjective standards. Generally speaking, if you get the unit you want according to your proper expectations, you have won the negotiation.

Sometimes an inspector will recommend a change that you have already planned on making. When this happens, remember the need to create a win-win situation between buyer and seller. For example, let's say you bought the property knowing that you were going to gut the existing kitchen and put in a new one more to your liking. Then your inspector comes back with a report stating the kitchen needs to be replaced. Don't use that information as a tool for further negotiation or to beat the seller out of a few more bucks. People do this, and it's as unfortunate as it is unfair. If you've planned on replacing the kitchen all along, the costs should have been factored into your price.

Sometimes people attempt to use the home inspection contingency to hold the seller hostage. Doing so could put so much pressure on the seller that the deal falls through. Even if the seller agrees and the deal goes through, such tactics could earn you a reputation as someone who takes unfair advantage of a situation. Word gets around. The important thing is to continually talk with your Realtor as things come up. The Realtor will let you know what's standard and fair and what would be considered taking advantage.

Some home inspectors play their own little games for their own little reasons. I've seen inspectors "find" normal and conventional things in a dwelling but present them as if they're catastrophic disasters in the making. A burned-out light bulb doesn't mean a failure of the entire building's electrical system. Invest the time to locate an honest inspector with a solid reputation, someone who will present an accurate report in a realistic way and will state clearly legitimate concerns and nonissues along with explanations.

Inspectors can turn nonissues into apparent catastrophes. Let's say you're buying a vintage building in an area where the land settled a hundred years ago. Let's say further that your inspector reports a hurricane is expected to land in Cincinnati on Tuesday, which means that the building will have some problems with settling before the end of the 21st century. You should know in this case that the report is about a nonissue; the situation doesn't require your attention.

An honest and qualified inspector will show you items that you may not know to look for. A wall that looks sound may actually be termite ridden. An inspector can find out by just sticking a pencil in a small hole in the wall. The soft sponginess of the wood indicates you should be told that certain wood elements of the structure may need replacement. If an inspector can slip a coin under a bathroom tile, you'll know you have to replace the tile on the bathroom wall. Lifting the wall-to-wall carpet in the corner of a closet may reveal the hidden treasure of a beautiful hardwood floor.

A good inspector can tell you the lifetime of the heating unit in your new home. A good inspector can tell you that your water heater is brand-new. A good inspector can also tell you that your water heater is an accident waiting to happen by noting that the rusted bottom means an inevitable flood, which could cost $500 to prevent, but you'll also have to cover the flood damage to your neighbor's unit if you don't spend the $500.

A good inspector is a good investment.

It's also a good idea to gain some personal experience in the arena of home inspections. Even in the best of situations, remember the ancient Roman warning of "Let the buyer beware." The ultimate responsibility is on your shoulders.

Start looking for a good inspector early in the game. I'd recommend you start compiling a list when you begin prequalifying. Check references and ask your Realtor about the inspector or the company's reputation. Hiring a home inspector lets you know what you are actually buying and that you're not going to face excessive repair and maintenance expenses once the deal is closed.

READ THE ASSOCIATION'S MATERIALS

The new condo, co-op, or townhome is your home, but you will also be living in an association, which means interaction with other members of the association. You'll be living under more rules and regulations than you would had you purchased a single-family dwelling. Make sure you understand the living arrangement you are entering.

Your contract should have a clause providing that you are given the association's materials and bylaws within a given number of days. It's a good idea to read them yourself, but it is essential that you also have your attorney read them. Make sure that you know exactly what you're getting into. Are pets allowed? Are grandkids allowed? Are there prohibitions on smoking? Can you put in an elegant wooden door? The wording of some negative clauses may be in legalese and without meaning to the average citizen. But to your lawyer, such language will stick out like a sore thumb. Any number of rules, regulations, or restrictions could have a significant impact on the quality of your lifestyle.

The contract allows you a certain amount of time to review the association's documents. If you need more time, have your attorney draft a request to the seller's attorney for an extension, which isn't an unusual request. The important matter is that you look, and look carefully, before you leap.

ATTORNEY APPROVAL

One of the best set of eyes to help you look before you leap is the set belonging to your attorney, even though on occasion I have seen lawyers muddy the waters so much that the deal falls through. As with hiring your home inspector, you want a lawyer who will give an honest opinion, look out for your interests, and act as a facilitator rather than a deal breaker.

The majority of problems, if they occur, will most likely surface during the attorney approval period. This is a set time frame, usually a number of days, specified in the contract that allows your attorney time to review the contract. It's a standard and important part of any good contract. The law, the boilerplate, and the legalese are almost impossible for most buyers to comprehend. Small changes in a word or phrase can have incredible consequences after the document is signed. That's why you need a lawyer—that is, a watchdog.

Your attorney should know that you want to buy the property but that you don't want to buy any unnecessary problems as part of the deal. The attorney may recommend certain contract modifications in your favor. These generally have nothing to do with the price, closing date, or contingency dates and can be easily negotiated with the seller.

Avoid the deal breaker. I have had transactions with attorneys who have actually killed a good deal for their client. Suddenly the attorney feels a need to make contract changes that have very little or no impact on the buyer. Perhaps ego takes over, or the attorney is trying to justify his or her fees. The reason isn't important, but here the attorney has changed roles—no longer an advisor but now a negotiator. It can happen easily, especially with buyers who are nervous about their own ability to negotiate with sellers. When that happens, you are headed for trouble.

I'm not trying to paint a negative picture of attorneys. On the contrary, most of my experiences and relationships have been successful and rewarding for client and attorney. But negative situations can occur, and I'd be remiss in not sounding a warning. I've seen attorneys get their hands on a client's paperwork and turn into a deal-breaking demon—to my mind for no apparent reason.

Always remember that you are the client. You are paying the legal fees and you are the individual in charge. If you have a question about your attorney's recommendations, then ask. If something doesn't feel right, find out why. Take command of the situation. Ask why a particular change is being recommended in the contract language. Ask what real effect the change will have; will it have any effect other than delay or deal breaking? I always say that if there's no real need or benefit in making a change, why bother making it?

Remember, most real estate transactions do not provide for recourse after the closing. The cost of hiring an attorney to pursue damages after the fact can be financially painful, win or lose. That's the value of finding and working with a good attorney who has your best interests at heart and will make sure that the dwelling you plan to *live in* is a deal that you can *live with*.

FINANCING

The conventional period for buying a property is usually 60 days. As mentioned earlier, you have about 45 days to get a firm and unconditional mortgage guarantee with the closing taking place within about another 10 days or so. Two months may sound like a lot of time, but the days fly by and a lot happens during those fly-bys. Everything has to fall in place in time or the deal falls apart.

As you begin writing your contract and initiate negotiations with the seller, you should already be prequalified to obtain financing. As I indicated earlier, prequalifying is one of the first steps you should take in buying property. You have those 45 days in which to do so, and the earlier you make your arrangements, the better. This time frame allows your lender time to make a formal application, submit the contract, verify your income, examine your tax returns for the past two or three years, see what deposits you have in local banks, check your credit report, and seek any other information the lender deems necessary.

Your Realtor will probably work with a mortgage broker or community bank, an institution where you are known and where you have already provided some financial documentation so that the process can move along smoothly and quickly. Believe me, you don't want to be near the end of the process only to discover there's a delay in your financing.

The standard 60 days for buying property isn't an inflexible rule. The actual time frame can be longer or shorter if all parties are in agreement. Sometimes it's better to take the longer course. Certain things that may not have been revealed early in the transaction may rear their ugly little heads as you move into the later stages. "Oh, did we mention that the basement is haunted?"

To me the most important element in dealing with financing is to know if and when you need to extend your contingency. If you need another two weeks, ask for them. Actually, this should be the rule with any of your contingencies. If you need an extension, get it. *Ask for extensions at least ten days prior to the contingency expiration date.* You're much better off asking for things earlier than later. If a deadline has passed, there just may be no later. By the time you've asked your attorney to request an extension and your attorney has drafted the request and by the time the seller's attorney gets it and discusses it with the seller, the contingency expiration date may be at hand.

Don't wait until the last minute to do anything—other than celebrate your new acquisition.

RENTAL OR SALE CONTINGENCY

In a perfect world we'd be leaving our old property on the day we'd be moving in to the new one. Everything would be timed perfectly for a smooth and easy transition from one dwelling to another. Is there anyone reading this book who believes we live in a perfect world? Sometimes you'll be ready to move into your dream home, but you still have a month on your lease. Sometimes you'll have three months, or you're living on a month-to-month lease with weeks left to go. Sometimes you're ready to buy a new home but have to sell the one you currently own and live in to finance the move. Whatever the case, you may need to deal with a rental or sales contingency in your contract.

In this situation the rental or sales contingency becomes a part of the contract as a term of the sale. The contingency clause gives you the right to sell your unit, sublet your rental or extend your rental lease, whatever the terms you need for rental or sale within a specified time. The language of the clause might read like this:

> This contract is contingent upon the buyer subleasing his apartment 60 days after acceptance. The seller will have the right to continue to show the unit and market the property, but convey to the buyer that he has received an offer at or above the buyer's offering. If this is the case, then the buyer will have two business days to waive this contingency or lose the right to purchase this property under the existing contract.

The most you can ask of a seller is to take the property off the market completely while you sell your home or sublease your apartment. Generally, that's asking for quite a lot. In a hot real estate market you might as well be asking for the moon. If the seller agrees, he or she will not want to deal with you exclusively without some control over how you are marketing your property. The seller will want to know that you've priced your property according to local market standards, how many showings you've had, or any circumstances that might prevent the sale from going through. This is fair. After all, the seller has a lot riding on the deal too.

It is normal and customary for the seller to place in the contingency clause the right to continue marketing the property. If there is another offer, the seller returns to you with a written and unconditional offer that you may meet or drop your contingency so that you can acquire the property. If you have this right and still need to market your property, you can close on the new acquisition without the sale's taking place. You should consider accepting this contingency so that you aren't paying two mortgages, or rent and mortgage, knowing that if the seller receives another offer, you can and will waive the contingency and accept the offer.

The risk you run, as indicated in the above example of a contingency clause, is that you might have to match a higher offer if it comes in during the contingency period. You may want to seriously consider avoiding any rental or sale contingencies so as to keep from paying this higher price. You may also want to alter the language of the contingency to indicate "Or Above Clause" so that if the seller gets an offer at the same price and terms that you've offered, you have the right to waive your contingency with no other charges.

Before inserting a rental or sales clause in any contract, discuss it thoroughly with your attorney and your Realtor. Make certain that the language says exactly what you want it to say and that your rights and privileges are protected. This situation isn't all that unusual, but each case is different and deserving of special attention.

* * *

Okay, so you found it, you negotiated for it, you acquired it, and you've moved into it. You have put it all together. But what about the person who hasn't found it? What about the person looking for a new construction? Well, there are pros and cons to new construction and that's what we'll be looking at next.

10

PROS AND CONS OF
NEW CONSTRUCTION

"You must have the ideas that have some promise in them . . .
it isn't enough to just have ideas, they must be finally
ideas worth having and fruitful."

George E. Woodbury

Many of the people I've worked with in real estate arrive at my office with the idea of purchasing new construction. For whatever reason, the thought of moving into an existing condo, co-op, or townhome is not part of their plans. New construction can be an idea "worth having and fruitful," but before making the final decision, you should take into consideration all the pros and cons. For example, if you're looking to move into a home by a specific date, you could run into scheduling problems. The unit, the building, or the development might not be completed by the date you want. If you are looking for a unit that you can customize and take the time to make it your own, then new construction is the way to go.

This chapter discusses a number of specific pros and cons of new construction, including special considerations in buying from a developer, the purchase agreement, the bylaws, the lease of the land if it's leased, and the development plan. But first I'd like to share a few random thoughts.

New construction will be presented to you in three basic steps. Step one is on paper, and there may be a lot of paper for a prospective buyer to read and review. You'll have the option of looking at site plans, blueprints, architectural renderings, brochures, flyers, and other promotional materials. This is the point where the buyer has the most flexibility because everything is still in the planning stages. Of course, some limits or parameters are set by the developer.

Step two is the construction phase, during which the development is partially built. The amount of flexibility you have in phase two depends on when you become involved. For example, you can't acquire a corner unit with a view of the lake if people before you have already taken those units. The earlier you enter negotiations, the more you can customize your purchase.

Step three is when the project is built and ready for moving in. Some personalization may still be possible because many developers specifically leave some areas incomplete to allow buyers certain choices so they can make the place feel like their own. Carpeting, wall paint, or countertops are examples of choices you may have even if construction is basically complete.

A plus for new construction is the builder's warranty, which in most cases is for a year. If problems develop during that year—a plumbing leak, for example—the builder has the responsibility to make repairs. Many tradespeople and subcontractors offer extended warranties for their specific work and materials. You'll want to examine all warranties carefully. Make a few inquiries about the developer, builder, and subcontractors too. You want to make sure these individuals and companies have a good reputation. Make sure they have the ability to come in and handle the punch list you develop during your walk-through and any warranty work that may come up during the warranty period.

New construction allows you to get in on the ground floor of a project in which prices will probably appreciate over time. Capital appreciation to your unit adds wealth to your estate. The roof over your head puts money in your bank. What a country!

Some vintage projects are considered new construction by most states and municipalities. A former large, downtown department store that has been gutted and converted into condominiums could easily and rightly be considered new construction. If you are buying into such a situation, you will still be dealing with warranty issues, new association bylaws, and assessments.

It's been my experience that when people have a choice between existing property and new construction they generally choose new. That's because in many markets the pricing of new construction is often competitive with, or even better than, the pricing of existing properties. You would think preowned dwellings would always be the least expensive, but that's not always the case, and certainly not a hard-and-fast rule.

I can't fully explain why this is the case or how often it is the case. But it's not unusual for developers to enter a market, tally up their expenses, and realize that they can offer homebuyers new property at a price competitive with the resale market. Builders have another strong advantage over the existing home market. As I just indicated, new construction means lots of choice, and that's a significant pro for buyers who have the opportunity to select colors and textures, furnishings, amenities, warranties, and other items that are unavailable to buyers of an existing property.

For me, the major consideration in buying from a developer is knowing the delivery date and having a good idea of the developer's ability to make that deadline. What happens if you make the commitment, sign the contract, and put down your money and then units in the development don't sell as quickly as the developer had hoped? What happens if construction then slows down or even grinds to a halt? What happens if you've sold your existing home only to discover that no new one is waiting over there at Slap Happy Acres? That's why it's important to have a bailout clause in your contract. If problems develop, make sure you can cancel the agreement and get a full refund of your earnest money.

I keep making one point because it's essential: do your homework. It's the best way to protect your money, your interests, and the quality of your lifestyle. Get a full copy of the property report, condominium declarations, and other materials before they are recorded with the local municipality. More than that, make the investment in time and effort to thoroughly research the developer and even the contractor and subcontractors. Make as sure as possible that everyone involved in the project has a solid reputation for good work, honest dealing, and commitment to customer service. That's the best way to assure yourself a smooth, hassle-free, and sound acquisition.

THE ADVANTAGES OF STARTING FROM SCRATCH

You'll discover many advantages to new construction, but I believe that by far the biggest one you'll encounter can be stated in a single word: choice. Very few choices, if any, are available to people who buy resale units. Of course, you'll probably have the right to make some cosmetic changes if you want, but they'll all be on your dollar. New construction offers the advantage of starting from scratch, often from the first scratch on paper of a designer's pen.

Choices include capital appreciation associated with new construction, cosmetic decisions such as colors and textures, amenities, and design initiatives. Do you want to live in a high-rise? Would you prefer a golf course complex? How about a community with tennis courts, health spas, and jogging trails? All these and many other choices are at your fingertips in new construction. Of course, the earlier you become involved in a development, the more choosing you can do.

PITFALLS OF NEW CONSTRUCTION

The greatest pitfall of new construction occurs when buyers find themselves working with a developer who "can't"; that is, a developer who

- can't keep the promises he's made;
- can't deliver the unit in the required condition;
- can't complete the items on your punch list or your finishing items;
- can't finish the job on time; or
- can't finish the job at all.

Working with such a dishonest or incompetent developer can be a hassle. It can become a major inconvenience, not to mention a financial and emotional disaster.

Such problems can be avoided by—what? That's right: doing your homework. Learn from the adage, "If it sounds too good to be true, it probably is." Make phone calls. Talk to people. Read the newspapers or trade journals. Get opinions from people in the business. Talk to others in the business community who have had contact with, or know of, the developers in the area.

Visit with your Realtor or find a Realtor. Be sure that when you interview a Realtor that neither the Realtor nor the company is affiliated with the developer. Realtors often have profitable affiliations with certain developers in an area. There's absolutely nothing wrong with such business connections, but you can't expect an unbiased opinion from a person or company with strong financial ties to a developer. Even people totally on the up-and-up can't refrain from being influenced by business relationships—that's just human nature. Seek out an independent expert who can tell you the pros and the cons of a particular developer or project. To be especially wise, you should consult a Realtor with no specific affiliation with a developer and one whose interests lie solely in selling you the property of your dreams.

I can think of a dozen developers in Chicago who, in my opinion, are in that "can't" category I just mentioned. Yet they continue to build, continue to have customers, and continue in failing to deliver on their promises. You'll find such businesses and businesspeople in every community, who stay in business because they operate on the "greater fool" theory—that is, regardless of how many people they fail today, they know someone who doesn't know their reputation will be along tomorrow. They keep selling because people keep buying without researching their investments. Your new home will probably be the biggest investment of your life. Please make sure it is a sound one.

A business associate of mine, a supplier of business services, has an interesting rule. He says, "I never try to sell a Cadillac to someone on a Chevrolet budget." That makes good sense. Applied to real estate, why try to sell a $1,000,000 condo to a family with a $250,000 budget? Unfortunately, some developers see things differently, trying to build a Taj Mahal in an area or community that doesn't require it and then trying to create a buying frenzy around the lavish development. Unfortunately, many buyers get caught up in all the excitement and find themselves the proud new owner of something way out of line with their expectations, dreams, and even their budget. Buying a home is an emotional decision, and emotion has its place in the process, frenzy is a poor emotion on which to base the biggest financial decision of your life.

Watch out for the developer who promises the moon. Again, if the deal sounds too good to be true, chances are it's so good that it's bad. Many developers building from the ground up, or even doing renovations, have presale requirements. They have to sell so many units by a certain date to complete their financing. Selling more units during that time frame is more important than any other consideration. Developers anxious to move quickly or who are in a financial bind may be tempted to offer you inducements now that they can never deliver on later.

You can avoid these pitfalls simply and easily. Find a developer with a proven track record, an individual or company with a good reputation in the community, and then work with that developer and ignore the others. That's not too complicated, is it?

LEGAL CONSIDERATIONS WITH CONTRACTORS AND SUBCONTRACTORS

Generally, you'll have no real involvement with contractors or subcontractors when you buy into an existing building. They will have been hired, managed, and paid by the developers, so working with contractors and subcontractors isn't an issue for buyers.

The situation may change, however, if you decide to renovate or redecorate your property. You may not find yourself the foreman of a construction site in this situation but you will definitely be a site manager. It's best to learn a little about the elements of your project and, more important, protect yourself in your agreements.

Obviously, if you hire someone to do renovation, restorative, or decorative work, you need to have a contract with that party. I certainly hope that it's obvious. Whether you draw up the agreement yourself or use one provided by the contractor, have your lawyer read it before you sign. Small shadings of words or phrases or subtleties in the document can have large consequences during, or even after, construction. It's better to have a pro look over any documents so that both sides are aware of their obligations.

Some contractors take your money but won't pay the subcontractors. Those liabilities can come back on you if you're not protected. If the project is a large one, it's probably a good idea to set up an escrow account with a title company. Remember that escrow is an agreement between two parties in which money is placed in the hands of a third party until the performance of a specified act is complete. This provides you some assurance that the contractor is paying his bills on time and the money is being properly dispersed to all subcontractors.

If the bills aren't being paid, it's possible for the subcontractors to place a lien on your property, which gives them the right to be paid on the sale of the real estate. It may also give them the right of foreclosure. Now, if you owe a small amount, say $2,000, chances are very slim that a subcontractor will endure the expense of a foreclosure. Still, why take chances? Write up a solid contract. These are the elements you want to include:

- Your right to terminate the contractor, provided the subcontractors do not perform
- Your right to remove a lien on your property
- A completion date
- Protection from the use, or a subcontractor's use, of substandard materials or workmanship

When dealing with contractors, beware the old "bait-and-switch" game. You know, that's going into a department store to buy an item on sale for a surprisingly low price (a price too good to be true) only to discover that the item is sold out. Of course, the salespeople quickly point out that there are lots of similar items available at a much higher price. The store baits you with the advertised special and then switches you to a more profitable sale.

Some contractors try their own version of the scam. Here's how it works. You contact, or are contacted by, representatives of what appears to be a reputable developer. The people look sharp, speak well, and seem willing to help you get into your dream home. The promotional materials on the development are professionally done and represent an ideal community, development, or building. This is what you've been looking for and you sign on the dotted line. That's the bait.

The switch comes rather abruptly and without your knowledge. Before the ink is dry on that contract, the salesperson you thought had your best interests at heart is down the street selling that contract to another vendor—the company or individual who will actually be doing the work on your project. Obviously there's a reason you're meeting with one company but will be dealing with another. Do you really think that reason is in your favor?

When drawing up a contract or signing a contract, make sure a clause is included that prevents the contractor from assigning your contract to another vendor. If you're impressed with ABC Company, make sure your contract stipulates that you *will* be working with ABC Company and not those blockheads over at XYZ.

CONSTRUCTION PERMITS

If you're planning renovation, restoration, or decorative work, find out what construction permits are required and then get them. I know, it's a "hoop" designed by bureaucrats who want to see you jump. Just do it. There are excellent reasons for those hoops to be in place, many of them more concerned with your health and safety than with any show of jumping skill.

Sure, it's a temptation to skip this little formality. You can always have a job done more quickly and for less money if you don't follow the codes set in place by your municipality. But that's penny wise, pound foolish thinking, and it can be dangerous thinking. Suppose you save a few bucks by using substandard electrical wiring. What value are those dollars if you wake up in the middle of the night to the smell of ozone and burning walls? Will you really feel like a smart guy who saved a bundle on plumbing when your bathroom becomes an indoor swimming pool? God forbid, but is beating the system worth it when your little construction project collapses on someone's head?

The small amount of money you might save isn't worth the financial and emotional burden you will probably pay later on. That flooded bathroom could leak into a neighbor's unit. The electrical fire could cause smoke damage all over the building. The collapsed construction project could cause an injury requiring hospitalization, treatment, and rehabilitation. Who do you think gets to pay for all that damage? These are serious matters, folks.

It's the contractor's job to get the construction permit, *but it's your job to make sure the contractor's done it.* It's your project, and although you may not be the foreman on the project, you have to take the responsibility to oversee it. Tell the contractor that you want a copy of the construction permit, properly stamped and dated, for your project files. If the contractor has a problem with this simple request, you have a problem with your contractor.

City codes are in place to protect the health and well-being of citizens and property owners. The rules and regulations help make sure that structures are up-to-date. The steel plating used in the Titanic, for example, was state of the art at the time but didn't stop the iceberg from ripping it to pieces. Your construction permit may not require state-of-the-art wiring (fiber optics, for example), but it will ensure that the materials used meet a rigid standard of proven performance and reliability. You can't say that about a contractor who says, "Oh, shoot, 'pardner,' we don't need no construction permit."

11

HOW TO DEAL WITH PRESOLD, UNBUILT NEW CONSTRUCTION

"Old is old."

Beatrice Egel (1925)

I've dealt fairly conclusively with the pros and cons of new construction in the previous chapter, but I want to make a special point, and it's an important one. *Everything isn't always as it seems.*

I'm sure most of you have walked into a show home on a vacant subdivision in or near a city. You've smiled at the salespeople, taken a handful of brochures, and looked at the designer's large and colorful drawings of what the place will look like in the future: clean streets, attractive homes, and friendly neighbors, all with your dream home right in the middle.

Others of you may have even walked into an air-conditioned trailer placed on what was once farmland or ranchland. You've smiled at the salespeople, grabbed your handful of brochures, and looked at the expensive 3-D diorama of an American Dream City. It's an aerial view complete with little houses, swimming pools, parks, landscaping, and other such amenities. It's an exciting visualization of what might be the future development of the agrarian land; serious buyers can be caught up rather easily in all the excitement and with good reason. But pay attention to the phrase *what might be* in the previous sentence. I didn't use it lightly.

DEVELOPERS ARE SPECULATORS

Speculators bet on the future, hoping that what they do today will offer a big payoff tomorrow. That's okay, and it's a cornerstone of the American dream. Every time we move to a new community, get a new job or promotion, or take on a new task, we're betting on a payoff in the future. *Betting* is a carefully chosen word. There's always an element of chance when anyone speculates, and some developers roll bigger dice than others do.

Developing a new community can run the spectrum from a hundred empty acres on the edge of a city's expansion to a small, in-fill neighborhood where existing property must be torn down before the new structures can go up. Either way, it's quite an undertaking and the developer must have some indication or a gut feeling at least about what people will and will not purchase. Getting the financing for a project often depends on a sound track record of achievement and the lenders' belief in the developer's ability to design, build, and sell the new community.

It's not unusual for the average homebuyer to think a developer has actually purchased all the acreage or property on which the development is to be built. In most cases that's just not true. Remember, the developer is speculating and may not have wanted to shell out the full amount of money necessary to acquire all the land. The developer may have only an option to purchase; and getting complete or merely additional financing may depend on how many homes or lots can be presold by a certain date. If not enough units are sold, financing may be withheld.

You should realize that even the best developers can strike out now and then. If not enough lots or homes are presold, and financing is not forthcoming, what then happens to the people who have already bought their lots?

Here's the entire point of this small chapter: know when the project is going to be built, how it is going to be built, and the precise time frame it will require. Please remember when you read all those colorful brochures, gaze at the colorful artistic renderings, look down on the 3-

D model of the new community, tour the property, speak with the sales-people, sign the contract, and write your deposit check, that *everything isn't always as it seems.*

BEYOND THE MOVE-IN

12

I'VE CLOSED— NOW WHAT?

"Here's another fine mess you've gotten us into, Stanley."
Oliver Hardy

You've written all your checks. You've signed all your documents. You've passed every approval, jumped successfully through every hoop, and have finally closed on your new property. Now it's time to unplug the appliances, wrap the dishes, pack the appliances, and call a mover. Well, that's certainly a priority, but there are other matters you need to handle too.

MAINTAIN YOUR PAPERWORK

When you close on your unit, you'll receive packages of information—paperwork. How many packages and how many sheets of paper varies from association to association. If you're a first-time buyer, chances are you'll receive a closing package from the developer that includes your condominium or the association declarations, the property report, and other related materials specific to your new association. In some cases you may have received these documents early for review by you and your attorney.

These are very important papers, so read them carefully if you haven't already gone over them. Don't file them away and forget them, and don't even think of "trash-canning" them.

These papers provide you with a budget or at least an estimated budget detailing association expenses. You will also have numerous other papers, documents, flyers, notices, and so on to help you understand your new environment. Remember, association living isn't like living in a single-family dwelling. You're a member of a closely connected community with specific rights but with specific responsibilities as well. It is essential that you know, understand, and adhere to these new responsibilities.

"But we've always had a cat" cuts no slack if you've signed an agreement to live in a pet-free community. Your 100-foot shortwave antenna may help you stay in touch with the world, but you'll have to bring it down if it doesn't adhere to the rules and regulations. Your need for a home office is irrelevant if you've just purchased a property that prohibits business activities. The other people in the community have rights too and they might not appreciate your customers (strangers) walking the halls or the sidewalks of their neighborhood.

You may find an association that is flexible or that looks the other way. It happens. But some of them are not only inflexible but have watchdogs out looking aggressively for violations. I've seen some associations make today's totalitarian dictatorships look downright benign. They're the exception to the rule, but they're out there, and that's another good reason for doing a lot of research before buying the property.

You will also receive your appliance warranties. Don't worry about the common elements; the association receives the warranties for them as they aren't your responsibility. Of course, you and the other members have a responsibility to respect the common property and not to trash, damage, or destroy it. Despite your cute little nephew's artistic abilities, he really shouldn't be given a handful of color ink markers and be told, "Go out and have a good time."

Regardless of the association, you will definitely be given paperwork, which may even include original building plans from someone in the association. If you don't get them, it's a good idea to ask for a copy. You will also get a copy of your contract, mortgage documents, and other items that relate directly to the sale of your unit, so you begin with a tidy pile of documents. This volume of paperwork may seem excessive or even unnecessary, but I assure you it's not.

PROTECT YOUR PAPERWORK

Every scrap of paper is valuable, and you should guard it as if it were a copy of rich old Aunt Jenny's will. If you have a safety deposit box with enough room, I'd put them in there. Also, I'd recommend that you keep copies of everything in two locations. Keep one set at home, preferably in a safe; but if you don't have a safe, you can purchase a fire-proof lockbox that can be stored as easily as you would a briefcase or large jewelry box. These lockboxes are reasonably priced and available in office supply stores and many discount chains. Compared with the consequences of losing your papers to fire, the expense is nothing.

Keep another set of copies with your attorney or accountant or some other place where they'll be safe. Wherever you decide to keep them, make sure that you'll always have ready access because you'll need them at some point in the future.

Everyone should read and understand the fine print of his or her contracts and agreements. I've known people who have studied their documents so well that they could have become the oral historian of the community or the rule- and regulation-quoting parliamentarian at heated association meetings. That's fine, but for most of us it's unnec-essary. Generally, once you've signed off on the paperwork you'll put it away and forget about it.

But, as I have indicated, you will certainly need those documents again. You and your family will some day want to move up to a bigger and better condo, co-op, or townhome. It's the American way. As some-one owning a unit in an association, you will one day be selling that unit. That's when you'll need all your paperwork because you'll be handing it over to the new owner.

KEEP OTHER PAPERWORK ON FILE

In addition to the paperwork I have just described, you'll need to maintain a file of other documents. These include receipts for work, repairs, and maintenance you have had performed on your property and notices from the association of changes in rules and regulations; certain association functions may be mandatory. It's important that you keep even simple notices and invitations to association parties, sidewalk sales, or other events in which everyone participates.

You certainly will want to keep a complete record of any correspondence you have with the association or officers and/or officials of the association. This is especially true regarding any disputes you have with the group or any member of the group. You never know when some event or action you haven't documented might come up as a point of contention. Having all your paperwork in order and readily accessible keeps you from falling into a "he said/she said" situation.

Whatever the case may be, whatever is mailed or handed to you or slipped under your door is probably an important document. If so, keep it filed away for future use. It may not be valuable only to you but to the new owner of your unit.

Saving the receipts for any work you have done to your unit is particularly important for sound financial reasons. When you sell your unit, you can add the costs of renovations into the basis for the price of your unit. You then have a higher cost basis and end up paying less tax to the government in the form of capital gains. Please, buy the fireproof lockbox and a bunch of manila folders. Organize your files, keep them up to date, and use them as the valuable resource they are when you need them.

MOVING IN

Every association has rules and regulations that are essential to assure a smooth-running association where everyone derives the most benefit possible from his or her membership. Everyone sacrifices a little so that everyone gains a lot. Some rules address the proper way for you to move in and out of your unit.

It is imperative that you read, understand, and comply with them. They're one of the ways to make sure you become a well-liked and respected member of a rather small community. People carry tales, and men are as guilty as women. You don't want to start your relationship with your new neighbors as a reputed troublemaker, which is remarkably easy to do, even unintentionally, if you don't obey the rules.

If you move into a high-rise building, for example, your paperwork may include a small document indicating a service elevator at your disposal. This elevator is available at all times and is even equipped with thick padding to help protect your property in transit. Now suppose you don't read that document and on move-in day your new neighbors discover the passenger elevator is jammed with your player piano. The line of people eager to go to work, shopping, or whatever builds up as you struggle with this musical obstruction. Frustration builds, the lines at other elevators stack up, and people are forced to use the musty and grimy service elevator. This is not how we make a good impression.

Townhome associations may request that you move in through the back entrances, and the hours during which you are allowed to move in may be restricted. It is your responsibility to find out and act accordingly.

If pets are allowed, you will probably encounter rules that address how you are to move your pet in and out of the building. Some associations restrict pet entry and exit to rear entrances. In some high-rise buildings you could be required to carry your pet in your arms in the elevator, a requirement that has the hidden benefit of limiting the size of pets allowed into a building without setting specific weight limits. Carrying Fido, the cute little bull terrier, for example, is no problem, but if you have a 200-pound bull mastiff, you'd better get a back brace.

RESPONSIBILITIES OF MOVING IN

Your move-in responsibilities, options, and restrictions will be carefully explained in your closing package of documents, your main responsibility being to follow them to the letter. If you're required to notify the appropriate association officer that you'll be tying up the service elevator on a certain date, then comply with that requirement. I'd do it in writing if I were you. Should you be required to use only the rear entrances, then don't try to sneak through the front doors. Basically, all you have to do is read the rules and obey them.

Other than that, I think your main responsibility is to begin your relationship as a good neighbor from the first moment you walk in. Regardless of what you're doing during the move-in, consider your new neighbors. You know, go easy on the shouting, don't swear out loud, try not to make excessive noise, go easy on the banging and bumping of furniture. Realize that others are already living there, so be respectful of their space, privacy, and peace and quiet.

Move-in is a great time to meet those new neighbors. Sure, you're busy unloading and unpacking, but if someone stops by to say hello, be courteous. Take a few moments to introduce yourself and get to know the folks you'll be living and dealing with for some years to come. Unless your arms are full of bull mastiff, go ahead and make the first move. If you see someone, smile and take a second to introduce yourself. In short, show your new neighbors that you're going to be a good neighbor and a welcome member of the community.

SPECIAL CONSIDERATIONS OF LIVING CLOSE TO YOUR NEIGHBORS

First, consider the nature of your neighbors: singles, families, retirees, or a mix of several types. You should have considered this prior to making your purchase to make sure you and your family will fit in and function smoothly as a member of this small community. Condo, co-op, and townhome living is association living with shared rights, privileges, and responsibilities. Much of what you do has a greater impact on your neighbors than would be true if you lived in a single-family dwelling for no other reason than the rules and regulations you must follow.

The key word in the above subhead is *close.* You're a lot closer to your neighbors in an association, generally living in closer proximity. You attend association meetings, mandatory functions, and other events. Participation is higher than it is in a typical block watch meeting or neighborhood meeting because every member is required to be there, and privacy therefore is limited. It's important that you realize, accept, and live comfortably with somewhat limited privacy. That's not necessarily bad; you get to meet and know a lot of good folks that otherwise you'd never encounter in a traditional neighborhood.

As a member of an association, you have a special obligation to maintain your property. You'll be selling it someday so you can move on to bigger and better things. But the nature of your environment means that the condition of one unit has a greater impact on the whole community than does the traditional single-family dwelling on its neighborhood. Each association has its own guidelines, but here are a few generalities that you can expect.

- Keep your unit well maintained and in good repair.
- Always check your heating system and air-conditioning system. Like the engine of your car, this is the most active piece of equipment in your unit. Keep the filters clean and have the unit cleaned and oiled once a year. This is also the most expensive equipment in your home, so don't wait until the temperature reaches above 100 degrees to realize that you should have heeded this advice.
- See that all appliances and amenities provided by the association are kept in good condition and good running order.
- Don't let your garbage or trash pile up. Dispose of it properly and on the specified days.
- Respect the common areas and act in a prudent and safe manner in them.
- Report any damage or wear to common areas. Some rules and regulations may require that you report significant damage to the association.
- Attend all required association functions.
- Provide documentation, such as repair receipts, as required.
- Abide by guest regulations, if any.
- Comply with any inspection requirement if so stipulated in your agreements.
- If home offices are permitted, comply with all rules and regulations governing them, such as limits on signage and walk-in traffic.

The best advice I can offer is the Golden Rule: Do unto your neighbor that which you'd want your neighbor to do unto you. Or not do unto you as the case may be. If you don't want to hear loud music coming through your walls, don't blast your music through theirs. If you don't like to experience rude people, then be polite when you meet a neighbor. If you'd like a little help with a home improvement project, volunteer to help someone else on his or her project.

Living with your new neighbors is really simple if you'll just use your common sense, basic good human nature, and willingness to participate in your community.

13

ASSESSMENTS AND SPECIAL ASSESSMENTS

*"Rules of conduct, whatever they may be, are not sufficient to
produce good results unless the ends sought are good."*

Bertrand Russell

Barron's *Real Estate Handbook* (2nd edition) defines *assessment* as "an owner's or lessee's proportionate share of a common expense" and *special assessment* as "an assessment made against a property to pay for public improvement by which the assessed property is supposed to be especially benefited."

As the owner of a townhome, condo, or co-op, you need to understand these terms because you will surely be encountering them throughout the period of your ownership. The first definition—assessment—addresses things, situations, and activities that are regular, normal, or fairly obvious. If you live in a high-rise condo, for example, you'd naturally expect to pay for your portion of the lobby upkeep, the elevators, hallway carpet, and so on. The following are generally considered assessment items:

- Insurance
- Water
- Landscaping
- Snow removal
- Maintenance
- Repairs

- Reserves
- Common area gas
- Common area electricity

Special assessments are a bit different. The need for them might not be so obvious when you sign your papers; for example, people don't really think their roof could cave in on them, that just might happen without proper repairs after major storm damage. As the extent of necessary repairs probably isn't in the association's budget, the money for them must come from somewhere.

The word *special* signifies that these costs are truly that—special or out of the ordinary. Other examples would be the need to repave the parking lot or parking garage; the need for your exterior brick work to be tuck-pointed when the association decides it wants to relandscape the property; or the need for the lobby to undergo a complete refurbishing to maintain the quality and appearance desired by the members of the association.

Special assessments should be rare occurrences, an important reason to make sure your association has and maintains sound financial reserves. If the reserves can cover the unexpected cost of repairs or maintenance, a special assessment may not be required at all. But if the reserves are inadequate, someone else has to foot the bill and that, folks, will be you members of the association. How much each member has to cough up depends on (1) the cost of the repairs and (2) the status of the reserves.

This is why I urge association members to carefully monitor the financial aspects of their membership. If your association's budget was put together with foresight and a healthy respect for all the things that can go wrong, then the association is probably building up a healthy reserve that results in less of a burden for members when a special assessment is required.

Please take extra notice that I used the word *when* in the previous sentence. That word was carefully chosen because it's not a matter of if you'll be called on for a special assessment; it's a matter of when. No association can avoid a special assessment requirement, which has to be part of the association's bylaws or membership documents. The need may not be now. It may not be for years, but at some time you and the other members will want or need to do some work on your association's property, work that cannot be covered by your existing budget.

THE NEED FOR ASSESSMENTS AND SPECIAL ASSESSMENTS

As mentioned earlier in this chapter, assessments and special assessments address very different needs—all are real needs, and some could even be urgent. The potential for the caving in of the roof comes to mind. Others may not be so urgent, such as repaving the parking lot, but they may be highly desirable and become a top priority. Financial responsibility, including paying bills, is the duty of the association, and that means all the members have a share. After all, that's the definition of an association.

In most cases a maintenance employee or team has the job of taking care of certain individual and all association property. Hiring a doorman for a high-rise building might sound like a luxury to some, but in many buildings that "luxury" serves many of the functions of a security guard at a gated community (another typical association cost). If your association includes access to a golf course, tennis court, swimming pool, or other expensive amenity, someone has to take responsibility for cutting the grass, purifying the water, mending the nets, and hundreds of other maintenance and repair duties.

Basic costs are certainly easy to understand. It's obvious that you need utilities, for example, but every association is different depending on its size, amenities, and physical structure. Assessments are merely a fair way to allow everyone to share the cost of running the association and maintaining the quality of life for which everyone joined.

Assessments are usually based on a percentage of ownership. Let's say you own 0.5 percent of your association; that means 0.5 percent of the association's entire budget is your financial responsibility. That's how much you own; that's how much you pay. The situation is kept equitable because larger units or people with larger percentages of ownership pay a larger assessment. You have to determine how much you can afford to pay when running the financial figures for the mortgage on your property—just another regular expense such as the mortgage payment, insurance, and taxes.

You'll be surprised how large an assessment can be when compared with that of another association. Comparison shopping is just as important when buying real estate as it is in the automobile showroom or the grocery store. Make sure you know what you're buying. If your building has the responsibility of supplying each unit with heat through one common area boiler system, then you certainly won't be paying for heat individually. You'll be making that payment as a group, and the cost of supplying your unit will be paid from assessments. The same holds true for water assessments.

Now you know why it's important to read your property report or the Realtor's statement describing the property. These documents state the amount of the assessments and what those assessments specifically cover. It's critical to know what your assessments *do not* cover—that is, the costs you have to pay from your own funds. The differences from one association to another might surprise you. Assume nothing. Read the documents and make sure you understand all your rights and all your responsibilities.

Let's return to the example of heating costs. Assessments may seem extremely low when both heating and air-conditioning are separate in each unit. If you are responsible for your own heating cost, for example, figures for that cost won't show up in the association's budget because it's not a shared cost, and it won't show up as a large assessment for your unit either. The low assessment you're looking at in documents has to be balanced with the fact that you'll have an additional expense in the form of heating and cooling costs. Again, you must know what the association brings to the table and what you have to bring on your own.

HOW ASSESSMENTS AFFECT YOU

Assessments have a profound and regular effect on you and your budget because you write out a check to cover them every month, and they are an important part of association living. You're responsible for paying your assessments just as you are your real estate taxes. They're not something you can let slide or try to talk your way out of paying after you've joined. I've heard people boast that "contracts are made to be broken." Perhaps, but I've seen more people than contracts broken by the effort to do so. As an ethical matter, you have made an agreement with these people, and it's your duty to hold up your end of the bargain.

As a practical matter, your association has the right to place a lien on your property and actually foreclose for delinquent assessments.

I can't emphasize how important it is that you remain current on your assessments. You must make those payments every month, especially important when you want to sell your unit. Before you can sign a contract, you need a letter from the association indicating that you are paid in full; without the letter you can plan on ringing up a big no sale.

After you've kept your payments current and you've closed the sale on your unit, you'll be looking for another one—and another association. I highly recommend that you have a professional or an expert take a look at your paperwork to see if the assessments seem too low for the new association. Notice that I didn't write "too high." Occasionally, a developer's greed or just plain enthusiasm for a project will overpower his or her better judgment. Assessments have been known to be projected at rates that could never cover the expenses of the association. Don't let it happen to you.

Later on, when expenses start outpacing funds, an association can do only one thing and that's reassess everyone at a higher rate. This may be little more than an inconvenience if you're financially sound. You may be a bit teed off, but you write the new numbers on your checks and move on. But you could be in for a financial struggle if you've maxed out your budget to live in that association. Making the higher payments could soon throw your personal budget off and cause serious hardship or distress.

This problem could happen to others in the association too. As a responsible member of the association, you don't want the group to have a difficult time from the "get-go" paying for its obligations. Assessments that appear to be low may just be a good deal. But you'd be wise to have someone who knows the business check out those numbers for you. As they say, if the deal is too good to be true, it probably is.

WHAT TO DO IF YOU THINK YOU HAVE BEEN TREATED UNFAIRLY

You address the situation. If you own a single-family dwelling and believe a neighbor is treating you unfairly, you may have to go to the police, the court system, or any number of civic authorities to handle the situation. The process could be long, complicated, and costly. One of the real benefits of living in an association is that you are not alone. Not only are formal rules and regulations in place governing rights and responsibilities of association members, but an equally formal framework is in place for handling problems. You have a board and an association that wants to maintain peaceful relations among the members and see that all members are treated fairly. The concept of a smoothly running ship is important in most associations.

Chances are you won't be treated unfairly on assessments if you're moving into an existing development. The budgets, assessments, and obligations have been proven over time, and there should be little need to experiment with them. You'll want to make sure that the seller of the unit you're buying has disclosed any requirement for a special assessment that may be on the books and looming in your future, as noted earlier, as you have a right to that information.

If the board had been discussing a special assessment and that information was not disclosed, you probably have legal recourse against the seller for nondisclosure. To discover after you've made your purchase that your new association is about to spend a significant amount of money, which will tax your personal finances, to repair, maintain, or make a change in the development is a significant matter. You should have been provided with that information before you closed.

Remember from earlier chapters that you have an attorney approval period before you make your purchase. Use it. Meet with the board president or representative of your new association to review carefully the rules and regulations of the association. Determine if there is any special assessment or other important matters you should know about. Ask specific questions and get specific answers. Legal recourse is always a possibility, but wouldn't you rather avoid the hassle, frustration, emotional drain, and expense? Well, you can, but you have to take responsibility for your own actions. And, as I just said, you can.

ARE THERE LEGAL REMEDIES?

I have often had to seek legal recourse in connection with my real estate interests. I don't like to take that route, but sometimes people and organizations leave you no other option. Although I'm not a lawyer and claim no particular legal expertise, I have observed the system at close range and found that when you have been lied to or facts have been misrepresented, legal remedies can correct the situation.

Deciding to seek a legal remedy generally boils down to a matter of expense. How much are you willing to spend to recover damages? Court costs and probably other fees are involved, costs that involve hard dollars. In today's complicated and ever-changing court system, lawyers are necessary and can be very expensive. Hourly rates mount up as hours turn to days, days to weeks, and weeks to months; I've known legal cases to drag on for years. You have to put aside your raging emotions and be objective and pragmatic. Will the end result justify the investment?

Another factor to consider is time. How much of your time are you willing to spend to recover damages? The old saying that time is money is absolutely correct. You will have to invest time gathering and organizing documents, meeting with your lawyer, making and taking depositions, and appearing in court. The time factor has an impact on you, your board of directors, and your association.

Your time has a dollar value, a specific hourly rate. Many people work according to an hourly rate and know that already. If you're salaried, simply divide your weekly earnings by 40 hours to know your rate. When you meet with your lawyer for the first consultation, get an estimate—even a guesstimate will do—of how many hours your type of case takes and multiply those hours by your hourly rate. That's how much your investment in time will cost you.

There's an adage proclaiming that winning is everything. I've known people who pursue legal remedies for lengthy periods of time at great expense. The time and money meant nothing to them because their focus was on winning at any cost, but I don't agree with that adage. I've seen instances when, in my opinion, winning wasn't worth the effort and cases where lawyers encouraged their clients to pursue damages much less than the legal fees paid to get them.

Again, I believe you have to put emotions aside before entering the legal arena. Perhaps you aren't seeking a remedy from the association or a member, but the association is seeking recourse from a developer or converter. I can guarantee you that one or more members will allow their emotions to rule their judgment. Some act from a sense of moral outrage, whereas others want "payback" or merely want to punish the developer. For these folks, winning is everything and they want to win at any cost.

Overly emotional members cannot be allowed to force the association into an irrational and costly decision. Calmer heads must rule at association meetings. Even if you win, is the cost of victory worth the time, effort, and expense? Suppose the judgment is in your favor but your legal fees aren't reimbursed. Suppose you don't receive enough money from the developer to reimburse your association budget. Someone has to be pragmatic, so the end cannot justify the cost, then the end sought isn't worth it. Sometimes the wisest course is to let something go.

This is not to say, however, that you should avoid legal action in cases of fraud, embezzlement, or misrepresentation. I'm just saying that you should carefully and unemotionally evaluate all aspects, especially time and money, before you make a decision. We have a great justice system, but it is expensive, time consuming, inefficient, and in many areas flawed. Lawyers and legal services advertise aggressively and often suggest that pursuing a legal remedy is much easier than my observations suggest. In our legal system, victory is never certain.

TRY PICKING UP THE PHONE

Because ours is a litigious society, often the first response to any situation is to call the lawyers and head to the courthouse. Lawyers are businesspeople, so when they are hired to do a job, they start doing that job right away. The hourly fees start right away too. My recommendation in most situations is to try to work things out before you involve the lawyers. Pick up the phone and find out what's really going on before you start running up legal bills. I've had experience in these matters.

While writing this book, I was the developer of a vintage renovation/conversion project, a great property that won the Good Neighbor Award for Excellence in Vintage Renovation Within the City of Chicago from the Chicago Association of Realtors. This project was a 15-unit association. I was waiting until all 15 units closed before transferring all the documents, paperwork, and everything associated with the project to the association so it could begin exercising its own autonomy—called a turnover. My experience has been that when you're close to selling and closing the last unit or last few units of a small development, it pays to wait an extra 30 or 60 days so that everyone involved has the opportunity to participate.

The final closing was on March 15, 2003, and the transfer was scheduled for April 24. While preparing for that meeting, I received a phone call from an attorney who claimed to be representing the owners of the development. I like living with a clear conscious and conduct my business with that goal in mind, so I didn't understand why an attorney would be calling me or why the owners would have called him in the first place. I was amazed because just two days before the phone call I had been in five of the existing owners' units with a Chicago Association of Realtors judge for the vintage renovation award. The owners could have addressed any problem or situation to me directly at any point during that time. No one said a word.

The attorney said that he had been hired by the owners to conduct a timely turnover of the development. Because the turnover was imminent, I couldn't understand why the owners would want to move up the date. The attorney wasn't aware that the turnover was to be so soon. He also questioned why the location of the turnover was in my office conference room rather than in the common area of the development. I replied there were no common areas that would seat between 15 and 20 people, which he wasn't aware of either. As the conversation progressed, I learned that the attorney was unaware of many important aspects of the building, the association, and the turnover schedule.

I discovered that the person buying the last unit had seen the attorney's ad in the paper and had prompted the association to hire his firm to force a faster turnover, which cost the association more than $1,000 in initial consultation fees. The average rate for a phone call to an attorney in a major metropolitan area is $250; a significant bill can result in an amazingly short period. The association had built up a nice reserve and had decided to spend some of it on unnecessary legal fees, but that was their decision. If a representative of the association had just picked up the phone and called me, those funds would have remained in the association's reserves.

I can think of many other examples of associations and their boards unnecessarily burning money in the reserve accounts. It's important that you, as an active member of your association, direct your board to carefully and critically look at the cost in time, money, and effort of pursuing litigation. Money that could be used for repair and maintenance or to cover a special assessment could be wasted in efforts that never benefit the association.

In sum, assessments and special assessments are a necessary and easily justifiable part of association living. They're critical for the enjoyment of your property, the maintenance and repair of the property, your pride of ownership, and the maintenance of a good quality of life. So every month when you write that check or the ACH transfer takes place, smile and give thanks to assessments for providing such a lovely place to live.

14

SELLING YOUR TOWNHOME, CONDO, OR CO-OP

When Is It Time to Sell?

As you have probably already guessed, the answer to that question: "It depends." No hard-and-fast rule declares the ideal moment to sell. The right time varies according to the economy, the needs and desires of owners, and the wishes of potential buyers.

Many variables influence timing. You may soon be getting married and need more room than that provided by your one-bedroom flat. Your employer might have just informed you of a new opportunity opening up across the country, and you realize the benefits of a quick move. You could just be tired of your present location. You might even see the wisdom of investing your money in property as opposed to monthly rent payments. Perhaps you've been reading the financial and real estate pages and have realized that your property has appreciated to the point where you should consider cashing in on your investment.

You should realize that the numbers are in your favor if you're interested in selling your townhome, condo, or co-op. Approximately one in five Americans move in any given year; that means 20 percent of the population is in motion and looking for a place to live. One of those places could very well be yours.

THE PRICE SHOULD BE RIGHT

Pricing your property to sell is a critical task. Note that phrase *to sell;* you must recognize market realities when setting the price for your unit. You may have hundreds of warm memories of people and events associated with that property, but you can't set a price on them. As wonderful as those memories may be, they are irrelevant to buyers. They don't have that connection, so you must factor that reality into your price. Sure, Uncle Bill may have told his wonderful World War II stories from that couch in the corner, but the new buyer doesn't know Uncle Bill and World War II may just be a subject covered in the history books.

Consult with a local Realtor who has a handle on the current real estate market. I've seen people sell out at a price far below market value. I've also seen people hold on to their property too long because their expectations were out of line with market realities. Either move can cost you a lot of money. Pricing your property right is probably the most critical task in selling it. Set the price too low and you'll lose profits that should by all rights be yours. Set the price too high and you may not see any profits at all because it won't sell. The guidance of a real estate professional can help you set a price that will earn a decent profit in a reasonable amount of time.

Whatever course you set out on, it's best that you have a well-considered plan in mind. You want your property to sell quickly and at the right price so that you can get on with your life and move on and up to your next property. You don't want to be saddled with a piece of property that's holding you back. The right time to sell is an individual thing defined by a number of variables. Major factors for one individual or family may not even be a consideration for other people. The real factor in any sale is what's right for *you*. Some people can afford to wait for top dollar, whereas others have to make a move right away and may have to settle for less. Keep in mind that settling for less than top dollar could be the wisest move for some people.

The key to pricing is the realization that the time to sell and the price of the sale are personal decisions with no across-the-board rules as guides. Think about all the factors that are important to you and your family. Whatever they may be, they will have as much effect on the time and price of your sale as will market forces, but please realize that ultimately the market rules.

MARKET RESEARCH:
ARE THERE ANY BUYERS?

Regardless of your business experience, educational background, and job title, you enter the field of marketing when you put a house on the market. It's best to work with a real estate professional who can guide you through this tricky area. He or she will put together a comparative market analysis (CMA) for you that is based on the ups and downs of your local market for the past six months as they relate to your type of unit. For example, if you have a 1,000-square-foot, two-bedroom, two-bath unit with parking, you'll be able to see what similar units have sold for in your geographic area. This information is invaluable in setting your price and in knowing an approximate time frame in which you can expect to make a sale.

If you live in a high-rise development, the CMA shows the sales that have occurred within your building. You'll know the selling price of properties north, south, east, west, above, and below you—prices that help you set your price. The sales within your own building are often the best barometers because the amenities are the same or similar. Those units make for better comparisons than units in other buildings, which have different amenities and are in (obviously) a different location.

A CMA allows you to compare apples to apples and develop a realistic picture of what you can expect when selling your unit. Not only will you get a useful guide on pricing, but you'll also get a useful idea of how long the sale might take. If units in your area are moving quickly, you can expect the same results—provided your pricing is within market norms. A CMA should be provided by your Realtor at no charge; the information shouldn't vary from Realtor to Realtor because all Realtors share the same information on which your report is based.

I don't advise trying to put together your own CMA. Sure, the Internet is a great source of all kinds of information, but the Realtors in any given area always have an edge, and it's an important edge. Regardless of how much information you can pull up on your computer, Realtors have more, better, more current, and more accurate information. They have access to local multiple listing services, which provide a staggering amount of current information. Even with access to the Internet, you just can't compete on your own.

Your Realtor is able to extract valuable information for you, and although it won't be specific to your unit, it provides an accurate average price within a certain range of what units like yours sell for. This is a priceless datum because it can help make sure you don't overprice or underprice your unit when selling.

Your Realtor should also be able to tell you if there are any likely buyers for your unit. The market time (MT) on the CMA also tells you how many days or weeks it takes to sell units like yours—again, invaluable information for making your plans.

I always suggest that you look at average time frames. Of course, local economies, location, amenities, and other factors have an effect on the price and timing of your sale, but a CMA still provides a sound set of guidelines. It's a solid base of real-world information essential to ensuring that you get the best deal possible for your property.

SETTING A PRICE

Setting a reasonable price should factor in your own financial and time frame needs with the realities of the local market. In a hot market, time and money are in your favor; when prices are depressed and units not moving very well, you'll have to adjust your price, time frame, and expectations accordingly. There are advantages to living in an association that many folks don't realize at first. One of them is that word travels fast; people talk, and they love to talk about the prices of units within the development. The grapevine can prove an invaluable source of pricing and timing information. It may be word of mouth, but it's also information that you can and should use.

In most cases, associations are required to provide you with a paid assessment letter to close your unit, and record the deed to the new buyer. This is simply to make sure that you have paid any money owed to the association for assessments or association fees specifically for your unit and to make sure that no money is in arrears when the unit closes. Guarantee this by obtaining a paid assessment letter from your association before closing. This letter informs the association who is selling a unit and also notes the price range of units selling in the local community.

You can't allow yourself to become overly emotional when selling your townhome, condo, or co-op. Let's assume that you have a two-bedroom, two-bath unit in which you've made wonderful upgrades and fabulous customized amenities. Moreover, it's full of happy memories. You have to realize nonetheless that it's still just a two-bedroom, two-bath unit whose wonderful memories don't exist for a prospective buyer. The value of the upgrades and improvements you've made are still governed by market realities. Those improvements might not increase your price as much as you'd like, but they should make the sale a little bit easier and faster and assure a little better price. Of course, this depends on how much the new buyer likes and wants what you've done. Again, market realities determine the final price and time frame for selling your unit.

Your improvements and changes have certainly enhanced your unit and improved your life, but the new buyer won't be looking at the unit with your eyes. The buyer will be seeing it for the first time as it is, not as it was before you made the upgrades, changes made to enhance *your* lifestyle and not necessarily important to someone else. In some cases, the prospective owners may not even care for your improvements and might even view them as negatives. Your expensive, beautifully crafted wall-to-wall and floor-to-ceiling bookshelves may be seen as an impediment by someone who doesn't read much. Home ownership is such a personal thing that when you're selling a home, or anything really, it's a very sound policy to put yourself in the other guy's position. Structure your sales pitch according to the other's needs and preferences. The buyer may not have much of a library, but perhaps those fancy shelves of yours would make an excellent showcase for the buyer's collection of old piggy banks, depression glass, or knickknacks. Put in that perspective, a negative can quickly become a positive and might even nail the sale.

Remember that initial reactions to your enhancements don't necessarily have to be permanent reactions. Ask questions. Get to know the likes and dislikes of the buyer and see how you can frame your changes in a way that will appeal to the buyer's lifestyle.

THE PROS AND CONS OF FSBO

I'm sure you've noticed those real estate signs with the letters FSBO on them, meaning For Sale by Owner, or "Fizzbo" as it's known in the industry. A lot of people are attracted to the concept of selling their own property because they can avoid paying the real estate sales commission. When you're selling a townhome, condo, or co-op, that commission can amount to a tidy sum.

Nothing is inherently wrong with taking the FSBO approach; you might be able to save a lot of money. But you should realize there are two sides to every story, and some things aren't quite as attractive as they originally seem. By taking the FSBO approach, you deny yourself access to one of the best tools in the real estate trade: the multiple listing service (MLS). This service, the first business-to-business Internet, allows agents and brokers access to information about the units for sale by all the other agents and brokers in the community. Agent John Doe on the west end of town has immediate access to all kinds of valuable information about the home(s) Richard Roe has for sale on the east side of town. It's an invaluable tool that helps move virtually every home that sells in any community. Some folks believe that the use of the MLS online service alone is worth the cost of the sales commission.

FSBO is practical *if you're in a hot real estate market,* in which case properties can sometimes sell themselves. Keep in mind that most of us aren't in a hot real estate market when we decide to sell our property; most of the time we're in a conventional market. Some of us are even in a depressed market and need all the help we can get to move a property, in which case we need the cooperation of Realtors and agents. They'll be able to screen buyers, weed out the ones who really won't be interested, and more quickly bring in those folks who would be most interested. A Realtor can look at the computer and in a few moments tell a potential buyer that yours is the right place . . . or that it's at least worth a walk-through.

Okay, so you still want to go it alone. You know you can post your sale on the Internet. You can print flyers and pass them out in the parking lots of the local grocery stores and malls. You can place ads in the local "penny savers" and stick brochures under the windshields of every car you see. That's all well and good, but realize that you're still shooting in the dark. The vast majority aren't even looking for a new house, much less your house. A lot of your investment in money, time, and effort is wasted.

The MLS, however, is targeted specifically to homebuyers' agents. It's the first source they turn to when looking to move a new property.

Without access to that marketing tool, your sales efforts could drag on for weeks or months longer than necessary, according to market standards.

When you take the FSBO approach, you cut yourself out of a network of hundreds, or even thousands, of salespeople who would love to move your property. Real estate professionals want to sell land, buildings, homes, townhomes, condos, and co-ops. Because they *really* want to make those sales, they're a resource you shouldn't ignore.

Also worth considering is that local Realtors may choose to focus their attention on other properties if you're not listed with one of them. Your unit may not be boycotted, but then again it might not be shown as much as it could be.

I'm not saying this is right or wrong; it's just the reality of the marketplace. A lot of real estate books encourage sellers to go the FSBO route or to at least negotiate a lower commission with their agent. Well, you can do that. No law says you have to pay an agent a set percentage. But I would like you to consider something. Most of the Realtors I have met have *earned* their commissions. They work hard at selling properties, knowing that the best deal for the customer is always the best deal for the Realtor.

WORKING WITH A PROFESSIONAL REAL ESTATE AGENT

A good Realtor will sell your property in the shortest time at the highest price and at the lowest cost to you. Of course, I'm prejudiced because I'm a real estate professional, and I'm also experienced. I've seen what happens when people try to go it alone compared with what happens when people work with professionals.

If you're considering selling your townhome, condo, or co-op, please consider the number of professionals you have at your disposal. Go to the National Association of Realtors's Web site <www.Realtor.com> or in Chicago log on to <www.car-Realtor.com>. By visiting these and other Web sites, you'll get an excellent insight into your community, your local real estate market, and the likely prospects for selling your unit.

There are people who "say," and there are people who "do." If you're selling a unit, it's important to find a Realtor who actually sells real estate; many so-called salespeople never make many sales. Look for a Realtor who has a good record of making sales within your neighborhood. These are the folks who will be sending you refrigerator magnets, calendars, packages of seeds, and other things designed to cement the bond between client and customer. That's okay. These folks will also be running through their list of prospects and weeding out the folks who won't or can't buy; these professionals will be diligent in their search for the right buyer of your property. They want the deal to go through just about as much as you do.

Evaluate how serious you are about selling your property. A lot of people want to sell immediately and a lot of other folks want to but can afford to wait a while. It's only fair to let your Realtor know where you stand, as a Realtor can do a much better job for you by knowing your real situation and your desires and goals. The time and talents of a good Realtor are not to be wasted or taken for granted. If you're not really interested in selling at the moment, let your Realtor know. Likewise, if you're in a position of having to sell right away, share the information.

A good real estate professional will always work *for* you and will have your best interests at heart. Just make sure that he or she knows the nature of those best interests. The time of a professional is valuable, so please make sure that you inform your agent about your situation up front. He or she will be able to do a much better job if you're both working from the same basic information.

Certainly, if you are a buyer there's no cost in working with a Realtor because a Realtor is paid by the seller. If you're a seller, however, certain legitimate costs are involved. Good Realtors are more than worth their commission. They're in touch with most of the buyers and sellers in the marketplace. They know a good deal from a bad deal and will do their utmost to protect you from financial harm. Of course, you are always in the driver's seat.

Sometimes it pays to provide your broker with additional funds to assist with your marketing efforts. The costs may actually help make your property stand out from the crowd and move a little faster than similar properties. This is a decision you'll have to make on your own, but I'd advise that you give it serious consideration.

The bottom line is defined by how fast you want to sell your property and how much you want to earn on your investment. Working with professionals in the industry is one of the best ways to make sure you get the best deal possible.

15

CONVERTING YOUR UNIT TO AN INVESTMENT PROPERTY

"Real estate value is historic. You just cannot buy today at yesterday's prices."

Mark B. Weiss

A family or an individual purchasing a condo, a co-op, or townhome generally has two courses of action in mind:

1. Living, enjoying, and growing in the property
2. Selling the property at some point to move on to another

A third alternative is also available to many owners and is directly connected to number 2 above. Why not turn the old unit into a long-term moneymaker instead of selling it? For many, the benefits of renting their property and becoming a landlord are very attractive. I'm a landlord. I've written a number of books on the subject and do a lot of public speaking on the subject. As you can imagine, I'm very much in favor of the idea, but I'd be less than credible if I said there weren't a few cons along the way. Let's take a look at the concept of rental property as it relates to association ownership.

If you buy into an association with the idea of renting your property as an option or even as a definite part of your overall plan, make sure the association rules and regulations permit it. Some do and some don't, and some are in transition to and from. If you think you might want to exercise this option later, make sure that it is available right now. If renting your property is prohibited, then you're clearly looking at the wrong association.

Many associations prohibit, or are very resistant to, allowing rental properties within the community. Why? Human nature. If people don't have an investment in something, it has no value to them. If they haven't paid for it, they don't respect it. I know there are exceptions, but as a long-time landlord, I know exactly what I'm talking about. A fact of life: Renters just don't care for their unit, common grounds, or the rights of their neighbors the way owners do.

Unit owners and associations have learned that fact the hard way. I'm not trying to be negative here, just realistic about the nature of my industry. Many associations that initially allow rental properties change those policies after unpleasant experiences with individuals or families with no real investment in the community. I've seen appliances destroyed, amenities ruined, and entire units trashed by people who, to outward appearances, were "decent folks." But troublemakers aren't delimited by income, race, sex, national origin, occupation, or education either. You can name any group of human beings you want, and I bet I can tell you of a rental unit people from that group have trashed.

Again, it's not group nature. It's human nature, and it's easy to understand. Why should the guy with the loud stereo worry about noise restrictions if he knows he's not going to be a long-time resident? The family with the young kids and a big box of crayons just isn't going to be as strict or as observant as the family with a financial and emotional investment in its unit, association, and community. That last item is especially important, because most renters aren't part of the community, don't think of themselves as part of the community, and never will be a part of the community. Association living is by definition a community of people with shared responsibilities. When one person doesn't carry his or her load, everyone suffers.

I love being a landlord and having the income that the business provides me and my family. I'm also aware of the hassles and pitfalls that come with the "trade." I'm just trying to alert you to some of the things you can expect. Hey, some of those things are pretty good.

EXCEPTIONS TO THE RULES

Occasionally you'll come across exceptions to the rule prohibiting rentals but only in extraordinary circumstances. An association, for example, may have a rule against rental properties but may still allow an owner to rent if (1) the unit has been on the market for a considerable period and can't be sold, or (2) if changes in the local market economy offer mitigating circumstances. If these exceptions are not in the original documents, don't count on talking your way into them later on.

Even if renting is permitted in your original documents, the rules and regulations can be amended. Even if your clear intent is to eventually offer your property as a rental and it's permitted in the original documents, you can still be legislated out of business at a later time. Realize going in that there's always an element of risk.

In some cases, an owner is in a position of being forced to rent the unit. Perhaps there's a serious illness in the family, and an owner has to move across the country. Perhaps an owner is transferred or gets a great job in another state. Maybe an owner has been injured and will require long-term care or therapy in a medical facility. For whatever reason, an owner suddenly has a unit that he or she can't use. The situation would have to be one of extraordinary circumstances, but it might be possible for an exemption to be granted.

You'd have to put forth a proposal to the association at the next association meeting so that everyone could vote on the matter. Remember, living in an association requires that many of your living circumstances or changes in circumstances must be voted on and approved before you can take action. That's the nature of the beast, and, as I've indicated, there are good reasons for association requirements.

Don't underestimate the need for, and the power of, politicking in getting (or not getting) your way. It may be a better idea to first make a personal presentation to the president of the association or to the board of directors so that they can make a recommendation to the association. Often when a proposal comes in preapproved from a board or the president, its passage, while not guaranteed, has a better chance of approval. It's as if the authorities have said, "Don't worry, folks, we've checked out this deal and it's okay."

A word of caution about too much politicking. Every group of neighbors is different, but usually one or more individuals are against almost anything and anyone. Some folks just get their kicks out of being obstructionists. Evaluate the people in your association carefully before you start knocking on doors; you could create more obstacles than you have at the moment. Again, the presentation to your board or president might short-circuit the problem.

READ RENTERS THE RIOT ACT

Better still, read renters the bylaws, declarations, and rules and regulations governing living arrangements in the unit, the common areas, and the association in general. Actually, you should make sure they have hard copies of *all* the pertinent documents. Many landlords have renters sign a copy signifying that they (the renters) have read and understood the agreements. The landlord keeps this on file in case a renter ever claims, "Well, I didn't know!" The owner can produce written proof that says, "Oh, yes, you did!"

It's sad to say, but many owners fail in this fundamental step, a real shame because everyone loses. Renters make mistakes that perhaps they wouldn't have made had they only known. While you're off in New Condo Pointe by the Sea, your former neighbors are suffering because of your tenant's lack of information. You could suffer too because someone has to come along and clean up the mess. Sometimes that mess is financial. Sometimes it's a matter of patching up broken relationships, and sometimes it's both.

It's important that you check out the rules regarding rentals before taking it for granted that you can do anything you want with your property. In an association you can't. If you enter into a lease agreement with a tenant and then discover that you are in violation of association bylaws, you'll have to terminate the lease, which can become a tedious, frustrating, and very expensive endeavor.

Even in the best of times and soundest of economies, a tenant may refuse to leave your unit. Unless you have a specific reason for removing a tenant, the tenant has the right to occupy the unit for the duration of the lease. Also, I've seen a lot of tenants remain in a unit after their lease has been terminated simply because they chose to be difficult. These are "holdover" tenants. Again, some people just like to be obstructionists; it may give them a sense of power, but the reason is irrelevant. You'll still have to file for a forcible eviction. That can be a long, painful, and expensive process, and you can expect the troublesome tenant to make you jump through every imaginable hoop in the system.

As a landlord, I see these and a hundred other problems every day. I'm economically and emotionally prepared to handle them. Of course, I'm a well-seasoned and experienced hand, but I've jumped through my share of hoops, too. I operate my business honorably and we comply with our contracts, preferring that the people we work with act the same way. Sometimes that's not the case, and we are prepared financially, legally, and emotionally to take care of any situation. If you become a landlord, some of these events may knock on your door (from the inside!), so you'll have to be prepared too.

Initially, however, the most important area of preparation is your association bylaws. You must know whether tenants are permitted in your building before you even consider becoming a landlord.

IS RENTING A SMART INVESTMENT?

People in America have an amazing variety of investments in which to put their money: stocks, bonds, oil and gas, precious metals, produce, and pork bellies. One of the most consistently popular investments throughout history has been, is, and will always be real estate. It's simply one of the best investments anyone can make, perhaps the best investment possible. That's not to say people don't make foolish real estate investments. They do, and even experienced professionals make mistakes.

I'm not going to go into considerable detail on being a landlord, as that would require another book. With all due modesty, I can recommend *Landlording and Property Management* (Mark B. Weiss and Dan Baldwin, Adams Media). Despite my obvious bias toward the work, it's recommended reading for anyone interested in the serious ins and outs of property management.

If you choose to be a landlord and bring renters into your association, certain standards should be adhered to for your protection. After you've advertised your property and people have started coming by for a look, you need to have two forms for potential tenants to complete: a rental application and a credit application. These forms should give you permission to check the credit, employment references, and personal references of applicants so you can find out whether these folks are responsible. They should have a sound track record of paying their bills on time and should have a clean credit record. Appearances can be, and often are, deceiving, so be sure to check out the details on the applications. Call those references.

The monthly rent should give you a small return on your investment as well as pay the mortgage and the association fees. You want a positive cash flow, not a negative one, which is to say that you want the money coming in instead of going out. You must ask yourself a key financial question: If a unit is vacant for a period or your tenant is late with the rent or not paying at all, can you make the mortgage payments to avoid foreclosure? Don't forget that real estate taxes are due on your investment as well. The real question is, Can you cover all the expenses, including utilities?

A unit will work well for you if:

- Your association permits rentals.
- You comply with all association rules and regulations regarding rentals.
- Your tenant passes credit, reference, and background checks.
- You can pay your mortgage.
- You can also pay your association fees, real estate taxes, and other costs.

Even if your rental provides you no cash flow, that's okay provided the rental covers your expenses. You'll still earn appreciation for the value of your association unit; and you'll still be making money over time. As an example, you can buy a unit for $100,000 and use the rental payments to cover your expenses as well as free up equity by paying down your mortgage over time. You could sell that unit for $120,000 five years later and have done quite well for yourself using other people's money.

I have a simple formula for locating an investment condominium. I ask a local Realtor to search the multiple listing service for the lowest-priced one-bedroom condo unit around. Then I buy that unit. The reason I work that way is because once you buy that condo, it is no longer the lowest-priced condo on the market. Even if you have to do some repairs, slap on some paint here and there, fix it up, and decorate it a bit, you then have a unit that can no longer be bought at that low price.

In sum, I believe buying real estate is a smart investment, a very smart investment. It's relatively low risk, and the potential returns are very good. As someone who has been investing for more than 25 years, I have found that real estate has helped me create my own wealth and a sound estate. I continue to invest actively and have no plans to stop.

When you own property, you are in control. You make all the decisions, and naturally, you'll make your share of mistakes as we all do, but that's part of life. Control is why I prefer real estate over the stock market, where you invest but have absolutely no say in what happens to your investment. It's all up to somebody else. With real estate, you know, or should know, what's happening with your property at all times. You can look at, walk around, and physically touch your investment any time you want. Sometimes the information you receive with stocks can be deceiving regardless of FCC regulations, as the recent Wall Street scandals tragically proved.

CAN YOU HANDLE THIS JOB?

One of the aspects of real estate ownership and management I love is that almost anyone can become involved and earn enviable amounts of money, and some of us do just that. You don't need a degree, a license, a trade school certificate, or even a high school diploma. Although I seriously urge you to educate yourself in the business and engage in continuing education, even that's not necessary. I've met people successfully renting condominium properties who range from blue collars to blue bloods, well-to-do businesspeople to starving artists, young people, middle-age folks, and retirees. If they apply themselves, work hard, and follow the rules, they'll all do well. Perhaps you'd like to join the family.

I don't have space in this book to cover even basic business techniques or the principles, practices, and pitfalls of becoming a landlord, but I do want to address one issue before you begin learning the business. Managing property is a business and as rewarding as it may be, it's a demanding business that's not for everybody. Before you make the commitment, make sure you have the basic business skills as well as the mental and emotional makeup to handle the job.

You need to have a basic set of business skills—how to keep books, for example. Naturally, you can hire someone to handle this and other tasks for you, but that cuts directly into your bottom line. You need to know basic recordkeeping and filing. Expenses mount up, and you'll need records for tax purposes. Insurance is a key factor and a major expense. The law regarding real estate not only varies from state to state and city to city but is always changing, so you'll need to make provision for keeping up with what's going on. A simple rewording of a single phrase in a city ordinance can have a dramatic impact on your business. If you're lacking business skills, check into your local community college or board of Realtors to see what courses of study are available in your area. Then study!

Government regulations and the mounds of forms and paperwork associated with it are another factor. Take civil rights legislation, for example. Suppose you have an interested potential tenant who happens to belong to a minority race. Well, that's no problem because discrimination on the basis of race is illegal. Sure it is, but what if the other members of your association don't want a minority in the community? There are all kinds of ways associations can discriminate without appearing to do so. It's happened, it's happening now, and it will continue to happen. Your association's racism (sexism, ageism, or whatever-ism) could prevent you from earning a return on your investment, which is just one of the challenges you could face. Do you have the makeup to overcome them?

I advise three things. One, build a support team consisting of an attorney, accountant, and banker. You'll need the services of all three during your real estate career, so don't fall into the trap of being penny wise and pound foolish. The cost of their services is far outweighed by the money, time, effort, and grief they will save you over time.

Two, get involved in your local real estate community. Find a real estate organization and join it. Attend the meetings and take advantage of the educational opportunities they'll provide. Network and get to know people who have been where you are. A conversation over a cup of coffee with an experienced pro could be of enormous value. Also, don't forget that networking is a two-way street.

Three, become a businessperson. When you get involved in real estate, you're involved in dollars and cents, rules and regulations, laws and the court system, good people and bad. You have to look at every business situation on the basis of how it impacts that business. If a tenant is consistently late with the rent, is abusing your property, or is creating problems with association members, you have to quickly and forcefully address the situation. You can't afford to waste time. You don't have to become a modern-day Ebenezer Scrooge, but as a business person, you do have to take care of business. If you're one of the folks not suited for this, becoming a landlord probably isn't for you.

CAN YOU HANDLE PEOPLE?

I believe it was Linus from the *Peanuts* comic strip who uttered the famous line, "I love mankind. It's people I can't stand." As a landlord, you don't have to love people; you don't even have to like them, but you will have to deal with them. People come in all types of personalities, from different backgrounds and with different needs and wants. Your rental is merely one stop on the way from here to there. You'll meet some of the best folks in the world and probably some of the worst. How will you react when your tenant calls up at 10 PM wanting you to chase down a mouse in the kitchen? Can you manage a situation in which an association member is threatening a lawsuit if you don't "do something" about your tenant? Will you be able to deal with a trashed unit?

A lot of problems your tenant will be facing, such as replacing a window pane, will be handled by the association or by the people hired by the association. As the landlord, *you are still going to get the calls.* You may as well learn a little human psychology, because you're going to need it.

FOUR TYPES OF PEOPLE

Every human on the planet has his or her own personality, but every personality falls into one of four basic categories. Despite shadings and mixings, one of these types will dominate. Renters come in all shapes, sizes, personalities, races, creeds, and colors. Still, after a bit of experience you'll find each one falls into one of five basic categories. As a landlord, you will have to deal with these different personality types. Someone who is highly analytical should be dealt with differently from someone who is highly emotional. You'll have to learn these types, learn to recognize them, and learn how to effectively work with them to reach your full potential as an effective landlord.

The first step is to figure out which is *your* dominant personality. You'll need to adjust your approach to each person, and you can't do that until you know . . . you. If you do any reading about personality, and you should, you'll soon discover different writers have different labels for different personality types, but all describe the same thing. Here are the four basic personality types of the human race:

1. *Analyst.* Analysts want to get in, get the job done, and move on. They tend to be focused on the here and now. A friendly chat might be possible but only after you've concluded the task at hand.
2. *Motivator.* This is a "get up and go type" who likes to be in charge. They make good negotiators, so be careful in your dealings. They're not necessarily dishonest but just focused, and you might give away the farm before you realize it.
3. *Neighbor.* Neighbors are friendly and easygoing people oriented toward building and maintaining relationships. Treated well, they make loyal tenants.
4. *Artist.* This individual is expressive and may actually be an artist or at least have artistic talents. Artist types tend to be chatty, friendly, and spontaneous, some of them tending to be even a bit flighty. You can certainly have a friendly chat with an artist personality; escaping that conversation, well, that's another story.

It's important to recognize these types and adjust your approach, appeals, and directives accordingly. Don't for a second feel that you're being two-faced in doing so. You're just adapting every business approach to achieve the best outcome for all concerned.

FIVE TYPES OF RENTERS

Just as there are four personality types, there are five types of renters. Naturally, you can have problems with anyone, but as a rule you can work rather easily with three of them. The other two types are troublemakers. Let's see what you'll be working with or against.

1. *Watchdog.* As I note in my speeches, seminars, and books, the term *watchdog* refers to the tenant who is always on the lookout

for problems or even potential problems. "Looks like that old window pane is about to pop out." To me, that's not really a complaint; it's information I need. I want to maintain a sound property so that my investment remains sound. I also want happy tenants, so even if I have to make a call to the maintenance person that the tenant could just as easily make, it's no trouble at all. I'm always trying to build and maintain a win-win situation.

2. *Whiner.* Remember that obnoxious couple on the old *Saturday Night Live* show who whined about *everything?* Well, there's a good chance you'll get to meet their real-life counterparts. It's important to realize that whiners whine for the sheer pleasure of whining. Their complaints may or may not be legitimate, but that doesn't matter because the purpose of their calls is to whine. This isn't all bad, for sometimes they call about real problems, and you'll want to see problems solved. Whiners require a bit of direction up front so that they know the parameters of when they can and cannot whine on your time.

3. *Victim.* This person is often without a clue. Nothing ever works. Nothing ever can work. You've heard about the person complaining that the television is broken only to be told that you have to plug it in first. Well, that person is a victim. You'd be amazed at how little a victim knows of life's basics. You have to be very careful with victims, or you will quickly become a babysitter.

All of the above types can be managed easily provided you let them know where they (and you) stand. Tell them what you will do and what they are expected to do on their own. You'll want to put a lot of this information in your tenant agreement. Go over it carefully and make sure they understand the rules. Have them sign off on a copy you can keep on file. Now, let's look at the problem areas.

4. *Slow payer.* This person is exactly as described. Oh, you'll eventually get your money, but you'll have to jump through all kinds of hoops to get it. I don't understand the reason behind it, but slow payers generally make regular payments. They're just slow. They get behind, set up a rhythm, and then stick to it. My attitude is that regular money is good money, so I generally go along. I do charge a late penalty for the inconvenience.

5. *Nonpayers.* This is your worst nightmare. There's no give with a nonpayer, so it's extremely important that you put on your business hat and take immediate action. Set in motion whatever steps are legal and proper in your community to address the situation. Because the nonpayer has no give, neither should you. You're running a business, not a homeless shelter.

FIND A REAL ESTATE MENTOR

One of the smartest career moves you can make is to find someone in the business that can show you the ropes, which is a lot easier than it sounds. All you have to do is ask. Most people would be flattered at the attention. If you are turned down, don't be discouraged; someone who is too busy or isn't interested wouldn't be a very good mentor anyway. Move on, look around, and ask someone else; you'll discover lots of potential mentors in every community.

Ask around. Find out who knows the business and the market and has a good reputation for honesty and following through on promises. Be selective; you don't want just anyone in real estate. You'll encounter a lot of part-timers, dabblers, burn-out cases, and people down on life. You want someone who, like me, is excited every day about the challenges and rewards of this wonderful business, someone who wants to share that excitement.

Beyond your mentor, don't hesitate to ask advice and counsel of other professionals. Be polite and be careful. You don't want to abuse the privilege with a competitor or try to get free advice from a professional who should be paid. But, in general, if you have a basic question, plenty of people will gladly provide a basic answer.

* * *

When it's time to sell your unit and move on, you have the option of becoming a landlord. Is taking that option a smart move? Only you can say. I definitely urge you to at least consider the option. Evaluate your business skills or your ability to acquire them. Think about your people skills or the lack of them. Consider your temperament and willingness to manage the people, the paperwork . . . and the profits of becoming a landlord.

The bottom line: If your goal is to buy and accumulate units and go into other investment property, starting out with condominium rental is a good way to enter the market and start making considerable money in real estate investments.

$\mathbf{A}\textit{ppendixes}$

SECTION OF THE EVANSTON CITY CODE

Builders or developers in the village of Evanston, a suburb near Chicago, must escrow a percentage of condominium sale proceeds as a guaranteed reserve to ensure that funds are available after closings. The funds are not returned until developers' warranties have expired and the developers have met all warranty obligations to tenants. (See Chapter 2.) This is the applicable portion of the city code:

> To assure compliance with the warranties set forth in this Section, the declarant shall set up escrows or other appropriate security acceptable to the City pursuant to the regulations promulgated under this Section, which shall provide for said escrows or other security to revert to sole control of the declarant at the expiration of the different warranty periods unless outstanding claims exist against them. Escrows or other appropriate security shall be in an amount constituting the total of one percent (1%) of the sales price of each unit sold and shall be a combined joint fund available for both common element warranty work or unit warranty work and shall be irrevocable until the expiration of the common element warranty period or unit warranty period, whichever occurs later. (Ord. 36-0-80)

WORKING WITH REAL ESTATE PROFESSIONALS

A business associate of mine is an avid hiker in the rugged desert mountains of Arizona. He told me that a couple of survivalists from the Northwest recently came south to test themselves against the Superstition Mountains. The men were exceptionally experienced outdoorsmen used to living for weeks at a time in the tall timbers and cool mountains, and they were confident of their abilities to handle anything the desert trails would show them.

Their weekend stroll turned into a five-day ordeal as they hiked, lost, back and forth on a rocky trail through the heat, rock, cactus, rattlesnakes, and scorpions. Finally, a hiker found the desperate pair and led them to the trailhead. My associate points out that the entire time of their ordeal they were within two miles of a major highway. Three out of four directions would have taken them to civilization in a short period. Had they climbed any number of short hills, they could have seen the highway and nearby homes and businesses; and they could have heard the rush of traffic or the noise of a ghost town tourist attraction in the area. Yet they were in unfamiliar territory and remained completely lost and in danger of serious illness, injury, or worse.

I hope you get my point as it relates to real estate. If you're buying a condo, co-op, or townhome, you need an experienced guide.

THE PERILS OF GOING IT ALONE

The perils of buying are too numerous to mention, but I'll address two of them. The first is the *property* you want to buy. The second is all the *paperwork* you'll face. Each is fraught with potential danger, and I don't use the word *danger* lightly.

Consider the property you'd love to buy—your dream house. Real estate professionals know the city, the neighborhoods, the builders and developers, and the trends. They have far more information than most people could possibly acquire—up-to-date information. After meeting with a Realtor, you will learn that the Realtor can select neighborhoods and homes that match your expressed desires. After each walk-through, you can cull the rejects until you have a short list of possible purchases. A significant factor here is the amount of time the professional can save you. On your own, you'll be looking at a lot more of those rejects and spending time that should be invested looking at more likely prospects. At the same time you're looking at an inappropriate property, someone could be buying your dream home down the street.

A professional who knows the trends can warn you of a neighborhood that is headed for a decline or can point out that the city has just rezoned the area, resulting in a goat cheese processing plant's moving in next year. A professional can also point out diamonds in the rough that the average buyer might pass by. You could miss a great home and a great investment simply because you don't have the expertise to recognize its potential.

That brings up another good point. Before you finalize your purchase, your home should be examined by a professional inspector even though a real estate professional's experienced eye is equally valuable in the early stages. A Realtor knows enough to spot some of the more obvious signs of trouble or potential trouble. Sure, your inspector would catch such problems later on, but why waste all that time when you can have a knowledgeable pro at your side from the beginning?

Paperwork, the second peril of going it alone, can be a nightmare for the inexperienced, and inexperienced describes just about every homebuyer in the country. You'll face a mound of legal and official paperwork: the contract for the home, a title search, mortgage loan papers, credit reports, association bylaws, declarations, rules and regulations, notices, and so on and so on. Many of these documents are written by and for attorneys and accountants, so unless you are a member of one of those professions, you must have professional and experienced guidance. When you sign documents, you are signing legal and binding agreements and can't come back later with a "But I thought . . ."

WHAT TO LOOK FOR IN A GOOD AGENT

You want to find a real estate professional with an *excellent reputation* who *knows the community:* the two big qualifications. A professional who has just moved to your community may have an excellent reputation in Chicago and that's great, but his or her lack of experience in the new community is a serious drawback. A local professional, on the other hand, who knows the community but is less than ethical will cause more problems than you'll want to face.

In addition, don't neglect the area of personal rapport. Regardless of qualifications, you need to have a good working relationship with your counselor. You don't have to become best friends, but you should feel comfortable with each other with a friendly and easygoing interplay. You and your real estate professional are going to be dealing with a lot of personal information, such as your financial status. You'll also be working together under some stressful situations, such as the negotiation for your new home. You don't need a pal, but you do need a partner you trust and with whom you feel at ease.

I think the key is to interview a number of real estate professionals. Too many people rely on a friend, a relative, or the first person who comes along. Sure, talk with those folks, but talk to a lot of others too. Ask around for recommendations. You know lots of people who have purchased homes, so inquire about their experiences with individuals and companies. Looking for a real estate professional is like looking for a new house. You want a lot of selection so you can narrow down your choices to the perfect one. This takes a bit more effort, but I promise you'll be glad you put in the labor.

TRICKS AND TRAPS OF THE TRADE: HOW TO WORK WITH YOUR AGENT

In a nutshell, work openly and honestly. You're going to be working with this individual on the most important purchase of your life, the individual who will be helping you make a commitment, not only of your hard-earned dollars, but of several years of your life. This is no time to hold back information.

Think of the search as a process. Every time you look at a property, especially the rejects, go over the pros and cons with your real estate professional. State clearly what you liked, what you didn't like, and what you'd like to see in the next walk-through. As you work your way through the process, your counselor will be able to find homes closer and closer to what you really want. Communication is two-way and you must contribute your 50 percent.

The purchase of a home is the largest expenditure most people ever make. More than finances are involved. You'll be living in, and growing a family in, that dwelling. The emotional aspects are considerable; it's likely you'll be living with the unpleasant consequences for a long time if you make any mistakes or errors in judgment. Please, take the time to find a top-notch real estate professional. I could list dozens of good reasons, but I'd rather you consider the bottom line. Make a list of everything that could possibly go wrong when you purchase a new home. If you go it alone, some items on that list will inevitably come true.

BILL OF RIGHTS FOR CONDO BUYERS

The Department of Consumer Services for the city of Chicago has created a bill of rights for condo buyers that I believe is a superior piece of work. I recommend it as a model for associations and association members everywhere. Here is the complete document.

A condo buyer has the right to accurate and complete information regarding the development.

A condo buyer has the right to receive a copy of the property report in easy-to-read terms and which contains all relevant information.

A condo buyer has the right to know what amenities are part of the project, such as parking, and which are not.

A condo buyer has the right to expect that all condo developments and renovations comply with all Building and Zoning Codes and that any and all violations will be corrected before the closing.

A condo buyer has the right to expect the developer to set up a bank account containing reasonable reserves to correct as required by State Law.

A condo buyer has the right to seek the assistance of an attorney who can enforce the condo buyer's rights under Chicago law and can seek attorney's fees for violations.

Advise buyer to ask for property report.

A condo buyer has the right to receive a copy of the property report upon request.

City of Chicago Municipal Code

CHAPTER 13-72
CONDOMINIUMS

Sections:

13-72-010 Definitions.

For the purposes of this chapter, the following words and phrases shall have the meanings respectively ascribed to them by this section:

"Blanket encumbrance" means a trust deed, mortgage, judgment, or other lien on a condominium, including any lien or other encumbrance arising as a result of the imposition of any tax assessment by a public authority.

"Board of managers" means the board of managers provided and referred to in the Illinois Condominium Property Act.

"Closing of the sale" means the operation transferring ownership of a condominium unit to the purchaser from the developer.

"Common elements" means all of the condominium except the condominium units. "Common elements" also include limited common elements.

"Condominium" means a form of property established pursuant to the Illinois Condominium Property Act.

"Condominium project" means the sale of or plan by a developer to sell or the offering for sale of residential condominium units in an existing building or building to be constructed or under construction.

"Condominium unit" or "unit" means a separate three-dimensional area within the condominium identified as such in the declaration and on the condominium plat and shall include all improvements contained within such area except those excluded in the declaration.

"Conversion," "convert," or like words means the offering for sale by a developer or his agent of a condominium unit occupied or rented for any purpose by any person before commencement of a condominium project which includes such unit.

"Declaration" means the declaration referred to in the Illinois Condominium Property Act.

"Developer" means any person who submits property legally or equitably owned by him to the provisions of the Illinois Condominium Property Act, including any successor to such developer's entire interest in the property; or any person who offers units legally or equitably owned by him for sale in the ordinary course of his business. "Developer" does not include a corporation owning and operating a cooperative apartment building unless more than six units are to be sold to persons other than current stockholders of the corporation.

"Offering" means any indictment, solicitation, advertisement, publication, or announcement by a developer to any person or the general public to encourage a person to purchase a condominium unit in a condominium or prospective condominium.

"Person" means a natural individual, corporation, partnership, trustee, or other legal entity capable of holding title to real property.

"Property report" means the property report required in accordance with Section 13-72-020 of this chapter.

"Prospective purchaser" means a person who visits the condominium project site for the purpose of inspection for possible purchase or who requests the property report. (Prior code 100.2-1)

13-72-020 Contents of property report.

A property report shall contain the following:

A. A statement indicating name and address of:

1. The developer and legal and beneficial owner, if different, of the land and improvements, including all general partners of a partnership or principal executive officers and directors of a corporation;

2. Interim and permanent mortgages or construction lenders secured by a blanket encumbrance;

3. The principal sales and management agents, attorneys, accountants, architects, engineers and contractors for the project;

B. A description of all property and improvements including the following:

1. Map, plat, or architect's drawing showing location and dimensions of the condominium project and the land it occupies together with all improvements, including recreational facilities, proposed construction, and present and planned location of streets and driveways;

2. The share of ownership of each unit in the common elements. The identity of owners of such condominium unit including the

percentage of former renters who have purchased or contracted to purchase a condominium unit when the property is a conversion, if known. If such units are owned in trust or by nominees, the beneficiaries or principal shall be named, if known;

3. A description of all of the common elements in the project, including a description of all existing and proposed recreational facilities, and other such facilities with the project. Limited common elements, if any, and their ownership shall also be indicated;

4. A description of the nature and ownership of all improvements occupying the same zoning lot but which are not part of the condominium;

5. Location, nature and ownership of easement streets and driveways on or contiguous to the condominium;

6. The identification of drawings, architectural plans, and other suitable documents setting forth the necessary information for location, maintenance, and repair of all condominium facilities and equipment, to the extent these documents exist, their location, and times at which they may be inspected;

7. Projected initiation and completion dates, for proposed construction, renovation, and conversion;

8. A description of limitations upon uses permitted in individual condominium units as contained in the declaration and bylaws of the condominium association and applicable zoning provisions. Such description shall state whether or under what conditions the condominium units may be rented together by the unit owner;

9. Statement as to whether a purchaser may purchase more than one unit and under what circumstances or conditions;

10. Statement of legal ownership, listing all restrictions, notices, lis pendens, and encumbrances of record;

C. Method of timing of transfer of control of the condominium to the board of managers and the nature and extent of any interest retained by the developer thereafter;

D. A statement disclosing the existence of penalties if the construction, renovation, or conversion or completion date is not met, and the additional costs to be imposed upon unit owners if such date is not met;

E. The nature and extent of any protection of a purchaser if the developer defaults on blanket encumbrances;

F. A statement of any litigation which would affect the condominium or the developer's ability to convey clear title;

G. A statement of the current taxes and estimated changes in the tax assessment of the condominium units which buyers may encounter during the first two years;

H. Copies of the forms of sales documents applicable to the individual units, including but not limited to:

   1. Basic purchase contract form being used by the developer;

   2. Deeds of conveyance;

   3. Deed of trust, mortgage, and promissory note, if any;

I. Statement of sales prices, terms, options, and conditions of sale of each unsold unit, including estimated closing and settlement costs and transfer taxes;

J. Statement of estimated monthly payments for each unit to be itemized as to taxes, utilities, operating costs, assessments, parking, recreational facilities, and all other payments in the first year after the projected date of assumption of control by the board of managers;

K. If financed by the developer, the proposed financing of each unit, including percent of sales price required for down payment, duration of the loan interest rate, service charge, appraisal charge, closing charges, and total monthly payment;

L. A description of all appliances and personal property included with each unit;

   1. Copies of the following documents:

      (a) The declaration and plat. However, prior to the recordation of the declaration, a preliminary declaration and plat may be supplied, provided it is accompanied by a statement in type size and style equal to at least 10 point boldface type as follows:

      THE DESCRIPTION OF UNITS AND PERCENTAGE OF OWNERSHIP INTEREST IN COMMON ELEMENTS HEREIN IS PRELIMINARY AND MAY BE CHANGED IN MATERIAL RESPECTS UPON THE RECORDING OF THE DECLARATION AND PLAT.

      (b) The articles of incorporation or charter of the condominium association, if any;

      (c) The bylaws and regulations of the condominium association;

   2. The description of the following documents:

      (a) Any leases of real or personal property in the condominium expiring later than two years after the first unit is offered for sale;

      (b) Any management contract, employment contract, insurance policy, or other contract affecting the use, maintenance or access of all or parts of the condominium expiring later than two years after the first unit is offered for sale;

      (c) The coverage and amounts of insurance policies applicable to the condominium, maintained by or on behalf of the developer;

M. A statement of management and expected management costs of the condominium including:

1. Name of management agent, if any, and the services the agent will perform;

2. Length of term of any management contract, its costs, and the circumstances, if any, under which the charges may be increased;

3. The conditions, if any, under which the contract may be cancelled or terminated;

4. A statement stating the relationship between the developer and the management firm and their respective corporate officers and controlling interests, if any;

N. An estimated operating budget, including the basis on which each item included in such operating budget was formulated for the condominium projected for a period of one year from the expected date that control of the condominium project passes to the board of managers. The operating budget shall include at least the following:

Operating costs
Utilities
Heating fuels
Janitorial services
Trash and garbage disposal
Ground and building maintenance
Security
Maintenance and operation of recreational and other facilities
Building insurance
Elevator maintenance
Sidewalks and street maintenance
Other operating costs

1. Manage costs
   Accounting and bookkeeping services
   Legal services
   Management fees

2. Reserve costs

   Reserve for improvements

   Reserve for unexpected repair work

   Reserve for replacement and upkeep of common areas and facilities

   Reserve for taxes and special assessments

If no reserve is provided for any one or more of the costs listed herein, the following statement must be inserted in the property report in a type the size and style equal to at least 10 point bold type:

THE DEVELOPER HAS NOT PROVIDED A RESERVE FOR CERTAIN POSSIBLE FUTURE COSTS OF THE CONDOMINIUM IN HIS BUDGET. ACCORDINGLY, IT MAY BE NECESSARY TO PROVIDE FOR A SPECIAL ASSESSMENT TO ALL CONDOMINIUM UNIT OWNERS TO PAY FOR SUCH COSTS SHOULD THEY OCCUR.

O. Provisions, if any, the developer has made to cover the proposed operations and maintenance budget in the event an insufficient number of units are sold;

P. If a conversion, a report from a qualified licensed engineer or registered architect describing the condition and expected useful life of the roof, foundation, external and supporting walls, mechanical, electrical, plumbing, heating, and structural elements and all other common facilities, together with an estimate of repair and replacement costs, for those items needing repair or replacement, at current market prices. This report shall include the approximate dates of major repairs to such facilities. There shall be attached to such report (1) a statement of the developer that no notice of violations of the building provisions of the Municipal Code pertaining to the condominium building have been received by the owner or his predecessors for 10 years preceding the property report and its latest amending or (2) a list of all notices of violations of the building provisions of the Municipal Code received, together with a detailed statement of all violations referred to in such notices, for the prior 10 years;

Q.

1. A statement of whether, and under what circumstances, the unit owners are required to be a member of, support, or participate financially in recreational facilities, such as but not limited to health clubs, exercise rooms, swimming pools, party rooms, and golf putting greens. If any such facility is not part of the common elements, the following warning shall be included in capital letters, in a type size and type equal to at least 10 point bold type:

THE (HERE NAME FACILITIES) ARE NOT INCLUDED IN THE COMMON ELEMENTS. THESE FACILITIES ARE AVAILABLE TO UNIT OWNER FOR (HERE DESCRIBE MONTHLY CHARGE AND INITIATION FEE). UNIT OWNERS ARE/ARE NOT (AS APPLICABLE) REQUIRED TO PARTICIPATE FINANCIALLY.

2. A description of the location, ownership, and availability to unit owners and the general public of accessory off-street parking associated with the condominium. If all of such parking facilities are not (a) part of the common elements or (b) divided as individual parking spaces among and designated as being part of the units, the following statement shall be included in a type and size and equal to at least 10 point bold type:

PARKING FACILITIES ASSOCIATED WITH THIS BUILDING ARE NOT OWNED BY THE UNIT OWNERS AND MAY BE SUBJECT TO BEING DENIED TO OR TAKEN FROM UNIT OWNERS.

R. A statement, if there are any restrictions upon the free sale, transfer, conveyance, encumbrance or leasing of a unit.

THE SALE, LEASE OR TRANSFER OF YOUR UNIT IS RESTRICTED OR CONTROLLED.

Immediately following this statement, there shall appear a reference to the documents, articles, paragraphs, and pages in the property report where the restriction, limitation, or control on the sale, lease, or transfer of units is set forth or described in detail.

S. A statement on the first page the following warning in capital letters, in a type size and style equal to at least 10 point bold type:

CITY OF CHICAGO LAW SPECIFICALLY PROHIBITS ANY REPRESENTATION TO THE EFFECT THAT THE CITY HAS PASSED UPON THE MERITS OF OR GIVEN APPROVAL TO MAKE OR CAUSE TO BE MADE TO ANY PROSPECTIVE PURCHASER ANY REPRESENTATIONS WHICH DIFFER FROM THE STATEMENTS IN THIS PROPERTY REPORT. ORAL REPRESENTATION CANNOT BE RELIED UPON FOR CORRECTLY STATING THE REPRESENTATIONS OF THE DEVELOPER AND ARE NOT BINDING ON THE DEVELOPER. REFER TO THE PROPERTY REPORT FOR BINDING REPRESENTATION.

T. The signature of the executive officer of the developer and statement affirming that the report and supplements, modifications and amendments are true, full, complete, and correct.

The developer shall amend the property report from time to time when any material changes occur in any matter contained in such reports. Amendments shall be made as soon as practicable after such change occurs or the developer has reason to know of such change. Amendments shall be attached to reports subsequently distributed to prospective purchasers and shall be immediately distributed to all persons who have purchased or agreed to purchase condominium units.

Not later than 30 days prior to the recording of the declaration and the plat, the developer shall give notice of any material changes in said declaration and plat as described in the property report to each person who has executed a contract to purchase a unit. (Prior code 100.2-2)

13-72-030 Misrepresentation or omission.

No person shall with the intent that a prospective purchaser rely on such act or omission, advertise, sell or offer for sale any condominium unit by (a) employing any statement or pictorial representation which is false or (b) omitting any material statement or pictorial representation. (Prior code 100.2-3)

13-72-040 Discrimination.

No person shall be denied the right to purchase or lease a unit because of race, religion, sex, sexual preference, marital status, or national origin. (Prior code 100.2-4)

13-72-050 Requirements for developer of more than six units.

A. Not later than the offering for sale of the first unit, a developer of a condominium of more than six units must;

   1. Have a property report available for distribution to each prospective purchaser and for examination by the department. A developer may make a charge, not to exceed $2.00 for each report so distributed;

   2. Make available for inspection by prospective purchasers copies of all documents that were filed or required to be filed in connection with the condominium project with the recorder of deeds of Cook County;

   3. Keep a receipt signed by each purchaser acknowledging that the person entering a contract to purchase has received and has had an opportunity to review the property report. Such receipts are to be kept on file in the possession of the developer for a period of three years from the date of signature of the purchaser and such receipts are subject to the inspection of the department at any reasonable time.

B. The board of managers shall keep a copy of the latest property report for seven years following the date of the property report's initial distribution. Upon reasonable notice the property report shall be made available for inspection by any prospective purchaser of a unit from a unit owner. (Prior code 100.2-5)

13-72-060 Notice to tenants of intent to declare submission of property for condominium consideration required.

A. No less than 120 days prior to recording the declaration to the provisions of the Illinois Condominium Property Act, a developer shall give notice of such intent to record to all persons who are tenants of the building on the property on the date the notice is given.

B. Any person who was a tenant as of the date of the notice of intent and whose tenancy expires other than for cause prior to the expiration of 120 days from the date on which a copy of the notice of intent was received by the tenant shall have a right to an additional tenancy on the same terms and conditions and for the same rental unit until the expiration of such 120-day period by the giving of written notice thereof to the developer within 30 days of the date upon which a copy of the notice of intent was received by the tenant; provided, that in the case of any tenant who is over 65 years of age, or who is deaf or blind, or who is unable to walk without assistance, said tenant shall have the right to an additional tenancy on the same terms and conditions and for the same rental for 180 days following receipt of said notice of intent to record by giving notice as aforesaid.

C. During the period of 120 days following his receipt of the notice of intent, and during a period of 180 days following his receipt of notice of intent in the case of any person who is over 65 years of age, or who is deaf or blind, or who is unable to walk without assistance, any person who was both a tenant on the date of notice of intent and a current tenant shall have the right of first refusal to purchase his unit. The tenant must exercise the right of first refusal, if at all, by giving notice thereof to the developer prior to the expiration of 30 days from the giving of notice by the developer to the tenant that a contract to purchase the unit has been executed. Each contract for sale of a unit shall conspicuously disclose the existence of, and shall be subject to, such right of first refusal. The statement in the deed conveying the unit to a purchaser to the effect that the tenant of the unit waived or failed to exercise the right of first refusal or had no right of first refusal with respect to the unit shall extinguish any legal or equitable right or interest to the possession or acquisition of the unit which the tenant may have or claim with respect to the unit arising out of the right of first refusal provided for in this section. The forgoing provisions shall not affect any claim which the tenant may have against the developer for damages arising out of the right of first refusal provided in this section, nor shall it affect the penalties provided in Section 13-72-110 hereof.

D. No occupied unit shall be shown to any purchaser or prospective purchaser for 30 days after notice of intent to record, as provided herein, is given.

E. Any notice provided for in this section shall be given by a written notice delivered in person or mailed, certified or registered mail, return receipt requested, to the party who is being given the notice. (Prior code 100.2-6)

13-72-070 Participation in recreational facilities not owned in fee by unit owners.

The developer may not require, nor, except as established by the board of managers following assumption of control by unit purchasers, may the condominium bylaws require that a unit owner be a member of or participate in recreational or similar facilities which are not owned in fee by the unit owners or by an association in which they are members, individually or through the board of managers. (Prior code 100.2-7)

13-72-080 Examination of records by unit owners.

No person shall fail to allow unit owners to inspect the financial books and records of the condominium association within three business days of the time written request for examination of the records is received. (Prior code 100.2-8)

13-72-090 Administration of chapter.

The commissioner of consumer sales, weights, and measures shall administer this chapter and may adopt rules and regulations for the effective administration of this chapter (Prior code 100.2-9)

13-72-100 Rights, obligations and remedies.

The rights, obligations, and remedies set forth in this chapter shall be cumulative and in addition to any others available at law or in equity. The department or any prospective purchaser, purchaser, or owner of a unit may seek compliance of any provision of this chapter, provided, however, that only the department may enforce the provisions of Section 13-72-110. In any action brought to enforce any provision of this chapter except Section 13-72-110 the prevailing plaintiff shall be entitled to recover, in addition to any other remedy available, his reasonable attorney fees. (Prior code 100.2-10)

13-72-110 Penalty for violation.

Any person found guilty of violating any of the provisions of this chapter upon conviction thereof shall be punished by a fine of not less than $100.00 nor more than $300.00 for the first offense and not less than $300.00 nor more than $500.00 for the second and each subsequent offense in any 180-day period, provided, however, that all actions seeking the imposition of fines only shall be filed as quasi-criminal actions subject to the provisions of the Illinois Civil Practice Act (Illinois Revised Statutes 1975, Ch. 110, Par. 1 et seq.). Repeated offenses in excess of three within any 180-day period may also be punishable as a misdemeanor by incarceration in the county jail for a term not to exceed six months under the procedure set forth in Section 1-2-1.1 of the Illinois Municipal Code (Illinois Revised Statutes 1975, Ch. 24, par. 1-2.1) under the provisions of the Illinois Code of Criminal Procedure (Illinois Revised Statutes 1975, Ch. 38, pars. 100-1, et seq.) in a separate proceeding. Each failure to comply with the provisions of this chapter with respect to each person shall be considered a separate offense. A separate and distinct offense shall be regarded as committed each day on which such person shall continue or permit any such violation. In addition to such fines and penalties, violation of any provision of this chapter shall be cause for revocation of any license issued to such violator or offending party by the city of Chicago. Nothing herein shall be construed to preclude the revocation of any license for violation of any other provision of the Municipal Code of Chicago. (Prior code 100.2-11)

13-72-120 Severability.

If any provision, clause, sentence, paragraph, section, or part of this chapter, or application thereof to any person, or circumstance, shall, for any reason, be adjudged to be unconstitutional or invalid, said judgment shall not affect, impair or invalidate the remainder of this chapter and the application of such provision to other persons, firms, corporations, public agencies or circumstances, but shall be confined in its operation to the provision, clause, sentence, paragraph, section, or part thereof directly involved in the controversy in which such judgment shall have been rendered and to the person, firm, corporation, public agency, or circumstances involved. It is hereby declared to be the legislative intent of the city council that this chapter would have been adopted had such unconstitutional or invalid provision, clause, sentence, paragraph, section, or part thereof not been included. (Prior code 100.2-12)

ENGINEERING REPORT
1334-46 WEST BRYN MAWR AVENUE

c/o
Mark B. Weiss, CCIM
Mark B. Weiss Real Estate Brokerage, Inc.
2442 North Lincoln Avenue
Chicago, Illinois 60614

as Manager for
BRYN MAWR AVENUE, L.L.C., Owner

Condominium Conversion
1344-46 West Bryn Mawr Avenue
Chicago, Illinois 60660

"LA VENTANA"

20 July 2000

Architecture Chicago Project Number 9902

20 July 2000

1344-46 WEST BRYN MAWR AVENUE

c/o
Mark B. Weiss, CCIM
Mark B. Weiss Real Estate Brokerage, Inc.
2442 N. Lincoln Ave.
Chicago, Illinois 60614

as Manager for
BRYN MAWR AVENUE, L.L.C., Owner

Re: La Ventana—Condominium Conversion
1344-46 West Bryn Mawr Avenue
Chicago, Illinois 60660

Dear Mark:

As per your request, I inspected the subject property on 20 July 2000. The following is a report of my observations relative to the current conditions of the structural, architectural, mechanical systems, exterior and interior areas, and site improvements.

General Conditions:

The property is improved with a three-story masonry apartment building with the basement spaces partially below grade, and contains a total of seven (7) dwelling units. The dwelling units are identified with the address numbers of 1344 and 1346.

Six of the dwelling units share a common "front" (south) entrance and "back" (north) porch stairs. The garden level unit at 1346 has a separate private front entrance. There is a common basement floor utility area in the rear (north) portion of the building. The common basement floor utility area includes private storage closet areas, gas meters, electrical meters and disconnects, and the water heater.

The building appears to have been constructed in the 1920s. There are two dwelling units on each of the above-grade floor levels, except the basement floor level contains one dwelling unit on west side and on the east side the basement level is duplexed with the first floor. Five of the dwelling units have two bedrooms with two bathrooms. The first floor east dwelling units has three bedrooms and three bathrooms, and the east garden level has one bedroom and one bathroom. There are eight (8) paved parking spaces adjoining a public alley at the north end of the property.

The basic construction of the building is concrete foundation walls under a brick masonry exterior bearing walls. The south facades are constructed of pressed face brick with limestone details. The north, east, and west facades are constructed of common brick with vitrified clay tile coping. The floor and ceiling joists, rafters, stairs, and partition wall studs are wood. The exterior brick bearing walls are finished on the interior with insulation between metal studs and covered with painted gypsum wallboard. The existing roof has been completely removed and a new roof has been installed. The new windows are double-hung vinyl with insulating glass and insect screens. Heating is supplied from new gas-fired furnaces in each dwelling unit, with supply diffusers and return grilles appropriately located. Central air conditioning is supplied using remote exterior condensers located on the roof or under the back porches.

It is my opinion that the building appears architecturally and structurally sound. The roofing, heating systems, plumbing system and fixtures, and electrical system and fixtures and devices are all new, adequate in size, and in excellent condition.

Site and Building Exterior:

The lot is a 50.00′ wide by 125.00′ deep rectangle on West Bryn Mawr Avenue. The rear (north) side yard is paved parking and space for refuse containers.

The original exterior masonry walls of the building have been entirely tuckpointed. All of the original wood windows in the building have been replaced with new vinyl double-hung windows with insulating glass. New steel lintels have been installed over the window openings in the front facade at the garden level. In all other window openings the original lintels have been preserved. The rear of the building has new aluminum gutters and downspouts and appear to be in excellent condition.

The main entrance doors to the building will be refinished solid wood with vision lights. The concrete entrance walk and stoop has been completely resurfaced with new material in excellent condition. The front and rear dwelling unit entrance doors are new insulated core steel doors.

The developer has completely recovered the existing roof with a new modified bitumen roof membrane and flashing. All new roofing surfaces should be in excellent condition. The new roof includes a manufacturer's standard ten-year warranty.

The original sheet metal cornice at the top of the front facade has been entirely removed. The masonry wall behind the former cornice has been coated with mortar and the wall has been capped with new limestone coping.

Apartment Building Interiors:

I visited the entrance vestibule and stair hall of the building. The vestibule will have restored original ceramic tile floors. The stair halls will have carpet over the original wood stairs. The flooring will be refinished existing materials with some areas restored with new finishes and should be in satisfactory condition. The walls and ceiling in the stair hall have been covered with a new gypsum wallboard veneer and currently appear to be in excellent condition. The wooden stair treads and risers and the landings are original construction in satisfactory condition. There is natural finished wood trim, door casing, and baseboard in the stair hall which will be refinished or painted and restored to a satisfactory condition. The steel apartment entrance doors are refinished with latch and deadbolt hardware.

The basement floor common areas in the rear of the building contain storage closets, water heater, gas meters, and electrical panels, meters, and disconnects. The walls and ceilings are new painted gypsum wallboard and existing painted brick. The floors are unfinished concrete slab. The ceiling and walls appear to be in satisfactory condition with respect to the nature of common utility space.

It is my opinion that the common areas, including the entrance vestibule, the stair hall, and the common utility areas, appear to be in satisfactory condition.

I visited all 7 dwelling units. All units are being remodeled at this time. The remodeling work includes new walls and ceilings finished with gypsum wallboard, new wood trim painted, refinished wood floors in the living areas and bedrooms, new slate tile floor in the kitchen floors, and new marble tile bathroom floors and shower surrounds.

The new walls, ceilings, floors, and trim should be in excellent condition. I am advised each unit will have new "Canac" kitchen and bathroom cabinets. The typical kitchen will have granite countertops, except in the garden unit there will be new laminate countertops. The typical bathroom will have marble vanity tops, except in the garden unit there will be new laminate vanity tops. Each dwelling unit will have new kitchen appliances (refrigerator, range and oven, microwave, dishwasher, disposal), a new sink with faucet, a new "stacked" clothes washer and dryer, and new bathroom fixtures (lavatory and faucet, tub/shower with faucet and drain, and water closet). The construction work in the kitchen and baths appears to be in satisfactory condition.

The developer informs me that all swinging doors within the interior of each unit will be new painted composite doors with new hardware, and all bi-fold doors will be wood doors. Each unit will be equipped with a smoke detector, carbon monoxide detector, intercom, and alarm system. New recessed and surface mounted incandescent and fluorescent lighting fixtures, switches, and outlets will be installed in kitchens and bathrooms in all units.

I am informed each dwelling will have a prefabricated, gas-fired, vent less fireplace installed in each living room. In my opinion, based on the condition of the work in progress in all units, the units will be appropriately clean and in satisfactory condition.

Utility Systems:

Heating will be supplied from individual gas-fired forced air furnaces located in the dwelling units. The supply air is distributed through sheet metal ductwork to supply diffusers.

All of the furnaces will be newly installed and appear to be in excellent condition. I have been advised by the HVAC contractor, Emex Heating of Chicago, Illinois, that all furnaces are adequate to serve each unit. The HVAC contractor has installed new ductwork to provide air distribution and accommodate central air conditioning. New central air conditioning will be provided in each unit with the condensers located on the roof or beneath the back porch. The furnace blower and ductwork provide the conditioned air distribution. The heating/cooling system appears to be adequate to supply heat for winter comfort conditions and cooling for summer conditions although the systems have not yet been tested in extreme weather conditions.

The plumbing system was replaced by Apollo Plumbing of Chicago, Illinois, and appears to be installed properly. The system should be in working order and in satisfactory condition. New gas service and distribution systems are being installed. All fixtures will be replaced and will be individually valved. I have been advised that all supply lines will be checked to confirm that there are no leaks in the system. The waste and vent lines throughout the buildings were being replaced with new materials to meet code. All plumbing work has been performed by Apollo Plumbing, a licensed plumbing contractor, and will be inspected by the City of Chicago. Work is still being done on the plumbing; therefore fixtures are currently not yet operational. Hot water will be supplied by a common gas-fired water heater located in the basement. The water heater will be newly installed and should be in excellent condition. The plumbing system currently shows no indication of leakage and appears to be in satisfactory condition with respect to the work being completed. Within the building, the supply, waste and vent piping is being replaced with new material. The kitchen waste piping appears to tie into an existing catch basin in the north yard.

The existing electrical systems are being entirely replaced by Kavanaugh Electric of Richton Park, Illinois. There is ample base-building electric service and there is a separate, new emergency electric service providing power to the building. Electrical service is separately metered for each unit. Each unit has a separate distribution panel with circuit breakers. All piping, wiring, switches, outlets, and lighting fixtures will be installed new. New copper conductors in new metal conduits will provide electrical branch distribution systems in each dwelling unit. The system capacity appears to be adequate for the proposed conditions.

Smoke and carbon monoxide detectors will be installed in each unit. In my opinion the electrical system will be in satisfactory condition.

The overhead service conductors running from the utility pole to the building appear to be adequately sized to accommodate the potential electrical load generated by the building systems.

Condominium Data Summary:

1. Structure:

It is my opinion that the expected useful life of the building's structural system should exceed (50) years if all elements are properly maintained and repaired as required. I anticipate the remaining remodeling work will be done as planned and will be in satisfactory condition.

2. Mechanical Systems:

The new HVAC systems includes new ductwork, new furnaces, and new condensers and appear to be in excellent condition. The expected useful life of the furnaces/condensers was estimated by the heating contractor to be (25) to (30) years with routine maintenance and repair as required.

The water heater will be a new gas-fired unit. The expected useful life of the water heater was estimated by the plumbing contractor to be (20) to (25) years with routine maintenance and repair as required. The water supply piping is all new copper material. The majority of the waste piping is new PVC with and some existing cast-iron underslab piping. In my opinion, the expected useful life of the interior plumbing can be expected to be in excess of (30) years with respect to the comments above and providing proper maintenance and repair is performed by the Association as required.

3. Utilities:

It is my opinion that the expected useful life of the major site utilities (sewer, water, gas, and electricity) can be expected to be in excess of (30) years, providing proper maintenance and repair as required.

4. Roofing:

It is my opinion that the estimated economic life of the new single-ply roof membrane covering the roof to exceed twenty (20) years with proper maintenance and repair as required.

Americans with Disabilities Act (ADA)

Compliance is not required since the subject property is not considered a "Place of Public Accommodation" and does not require adherence to Title III of the *Americans with Disabilities Act (ADA) Accessibility Guidelines (ADAAG).*

Environmental:

This report does not include any comments or responsibility with respect to environmental considerations.

My opinion is that the building appears to be basically structurally sound with respect to conversion of properties required by Section 100.2-30 of the Municipal Code of Chicago ordinance in that regard. It appears the work currently in progress has been installed in compliance with the applicable regulations.

My observations are of a visual nature. Material was not removed for observation of areas not visible. The scope of this assignment is limited to the survey type overview of the various elements noted above. I do not warrant the condition of, nor the work done to, this property. We take no responsibility for matters that are legal, questions of survey, or elements of basic design or engineering. If you or anyone who receives this report have any questions regarding the meaning or content herein, please do not hesitate to call me for clarification.

Best Regards,

Architecture Chicago
Wayne E. Zuschlag, Licensed Architect

Chapter 1

1. Industry Watch, "Condos Make Great Investments, Says NAR," *Realtor Magazine Online,* 4 February 2003.

2. D. Foligno, "Field Guide to Diversity for Realtors," Realtor.org, 23 February 2003.

Chapter 5

1. "Condo Market Shy of Record in Second Quarter 2002," Realtor .org, 14 November 2003.

2. Ibid.

Chapter 6

1. National Association of Realtors, Realtor.org, "High Housing Costs Are Changing American Lifestyles: NAR Survey," 4 February 2003.

2. National Association of Realtors, Realtor.org, "Downtown Living Remains Strong," 23 February 2003.

3. National Association of Realtors, Realtor.org, "Sheltering America," 23 February 2003.

ABOUT THE AUTHOR

Mark B. Weiss began the company bearing his name in 1988. Since then Mark B. Weiss Real Estate Brokerage, Inc., has taken a prominent role in the sales and development of real property, Through its successes it has become well recognized as a leader in the sale of commercial and investment property for private owners, financial institutions, corporations, and trusts, as well as a developer of vintage property renovations throughout Chicago's neighborhoods.

A graduate of DePaul University, Mr. Weiss is president of the Lincoln Park Builders Club, a member of the board of directors of the Chicago Association of Realtors (CAR), and was chairman of the Commercial Investment Committee of CAR from 2000 through 2002. He was a director of the Illinois CCIM chapter, a member in perpetuity and past director of the Chicago Real Estate Council, and a member of the National Association of Realtors and the Realtor's National Marketing Institute. He is also a member of the Real Estate Investment Association, the National Association of Bankruptcy Trustees, the National Association of Auctioneers, and the Lincoln Park Chamber of Commerce.

Mr. Weiss is a member of the City of Chicago's Building Permit Center Advisory Board and has received, on multiple occasions, awards for vintage restoration and historic preservation by the Chicago Association of Realtors in both rental and condominium buildings. He is a founder of the New Century Bank, serves on the holding company's board of directors, and is a board member of Ontario Street Investments.

Mr. Weiss has also authored *The Streetwise Guide to Property Management and Landlording* and *The Everything Home Buying Book,* published by Adams Media in Avon, Massachusetts. Mr. Weiss is a receiver in

Cook County and DuPage County and has often been retained as an expert witness in legal cases involving a variety of real estate matters.

Mr. Weiss has been actively engaged in selling property using the auction method of sale and is well respected locally as well as nationally for his successful real estate auction events. He is well versed in traditional sales as well as sealed-bid and public call auctions, and acts in the capacity of auctioneer as well as auction event coordinator.

Mr. Weiss often appears on local television programs as a real estate expert for interviews and panel discussions.

He teaches real estate classes for the Latin School of Chicago's Live and Learn program, and the Learning Annex in Los Angeles and New York City.

Mr. Weiss is the chairman of the Mark B. Weiss Foundation, which annually conducts the "Kindle the Lights" scholarship award. Charitable contributions are distributed to a variety of worthy causes from his foundation.

Mr. Weiss Can be contacted at the office of Mark B. Weiss Real Estate Brokerage, Inc., 2442 N. Lincoln Avenue, Chicago, Illinois 60614; 1-773-871-1818; Fax 1-773-871-2365, <www.markbweissre.com>.